Fast-Track to Your Next Job!

Fast-Track to Your Next Job!

The Complete No-nonsense Guide

Marvin Adams, M.A.

iUniverse, Inc.
New York Lincoln Shanghai

Fast-Track to Your Next Job!
The Complete No-nonsense Guide

iUniverse, Inc.

For information address:
iUniverse, Inc.
2021 Pine Lake Road, Suite 100
Lincoln, NE 68512
www.iuniverse.com

ISBN: 0-595-31885-1

Printed in the United States of America

Joan
My wife & inspiration

Contents

CHAPTER 1   INTRODUCTION 1

CHAPTER 2   COPING 3

- *THE WORLD OF STRESS* *3*
- *EMOTIONS, EMOTIONS!* *4*
- *SO YOU LOST YOUR JOB* *4*
- *"SO WHAT DO YOU DO?"* *5*
- *TIME FRAME* *5*
- *IT'S YOUR CHOICE* *5*
- *HOW'S THE FAMILY TAKING IT?* *6*
- *BUT NOTHING'S HAPPENING* *7*
- *THINGS TO KEEP YOU GOING* *8*
- *DANGER SIGNS* *9*
- *FIVE COMMON MISUNDERSTANDINGS* *10*
- *WHAT YOU CAN DO* *12*

CHAPTER 3   ASSESSMENT TOOLS 14

- *VALUES* *14*
- *TRANSFERABLE SKILLS* *15*
- *ARE YOU STILL NOT SURE WHAT YOU WANT TO DO?* *18*
- *PONDERABLES* *19*

CHAPTER 4   10 EASY STEPS TO A GREAT RESUME! 20

- *SUMMARY STATEMENT* *22*
- *ACTION VERBS* *24*
- *SAMPLE RESUME* *31*
- *COVER LETTER* *32*

- *SAMPLE COVER LETTER*. *34*
- *REFERENCES* *34*
- *SAMPLE REFERENCES*. *36*

CHAPTER 5   JOB SEARCH STRATEGIES. 37
- *PRODUCTIVITY*. *37*
- *MARKETING STRATEGY*. *37*
- *NETWORKING* *41*

CHAPTER 6   SURFING THE INTERNET. 44
- *META or MULTIPLE SITE SEARCH* *44*
- *GENERAL or JOB BANKS* *44*
- *SPECIALTY JOB BANKS* *45*
- *EMPLOYMENT AGENCIES* *46*
- *ASSESSMENTS* *47*
- *WORK AT HOME DIRECTORIES/RESOURCES* *47*
- *RESEARCH—INDUSTRY/COMPANY* *48*
- *COMPANY LOCATIONS* *48*
- *ASSOCIATION LISTS* *49*
- *MISCELLANEOUS* *49*

CHAPTER 7   JOB FAIRS 51
- *GETTING PREPARED*. *51*
- *ASKING QUESTIONS* *53*
- *THE FOLLOW-UP*. *53*

CHAPTER 8   INTERVIEWING SECRETS THAT WORK!. . . . 55
- *TWO MAJOR SECRETS*. *55*
- *PREPARATION for the INTERVIEW*. *57*
- *YOUR ARRIVAL*. *59*
- *OUTER OFFICE* *59*
- *THE INTERVIEW* *60*
- *QUESTIONS, QUESTIONS and MORE QUESTIONS!* *61*
- *I GET SO NERVOUS* *62*
- *TELL ME A LITTLE ABOUT YOURSELF* *63*

- *GET AWAY FROM YOUR RESUME!* *63*
- *STORY TIME* *64*
- *EMOTIONS WIN OVER LOGIC* *65*
- *ILLEGAL and INAPPROPRIATE QUESTIONS* *66*
- *BALANCE QUESTIONS* *66*
- *NEAR THE END* *67*
- *I WANT THIS JOB* *67*
- *THE EXIT QUESTION* *68*

CHAPTER 9   INTERVIEWING—Great Answers for Tough Questions **69**
- *INTERVIEW QUESTIONS in REVERSE!* *78*
- *THANK-YOU NOTES* *80*

CHAPTER 10   NEGOTIATING WITH EASE **81**
- *WHAT IS YOUR SALARY REQUIREMENT?* *81*
- *WHAT CAN YOU NEGOTIATE?* *83*
- *WHAT ABOUT EMPLOYMENT CONTRACTS?* *84*
- *SIGNING THE DEAL* *85*
- *IN SUMMARY* *85*

CHAPTER 11   HOW FRIENDS CAN HELP **86**
- *UNDERSTANDING UNEMPLOYMENT* *86*
- *WHAT CAN A FRIEND DO?* *88*

CHAPTER 12   TEN WORK MYTHS **90**

CHAPTER 13   DRESS & IMAGE **91**

CHAPTER 14   KEEPING TRACK **93**
- *MY NEXT JOB* *94*
- *ACTIVITY LOG* *95*
- *TELEPHONE LOG* *96*
- *POCKET INTERVIEW CHECKLIST* *97*
- *INTERVIEW SELF-EVALUATION* *99*

ADDITIONAL RESOURCES 101

About the Author 105

Acknowledgements

My thanks to Ken Wenzer for his encouragement, editing skills and belief that this book would come to fruition. Also, my thanks to Leslie Schwarzer for sharing her creative artwork.

1

INTRODUCTION

If you're looking for a method to help you find a job, you've found the right book. This all-in-one book covers all the subjects that you will need to find the right job.

Whether you're tired of the job you're in or if you been layed-off, searching for a new job is often a difficult and emotionally trying. This book is designed to assist you on your journey to a new job without making you into professional job developer. There are a lot of books on resume writing, interviewing, networking and strategies. But who wants to read an entire book and become an expert on some topic such as interviewing or resume writing? You just want a job.

This book presents the essentials and nothing more on what needs to be done to help you land the right job. You don't have to become an expert job developer in order to succeed in getting a new job. I've help place hundreds of job seekers. As a job developer I've fine tuned these techniques and strategies. I know these methods work. If you follow them, you will also be successful.

This book is divided into different chapters, covering different aspects of job hunting. Each chapter stands on its own. You do not need to read the entire book in the specified chapter order. For example, if you're interested in writing a resume you can go right to the resume chapter without having to read the other chapters. Or, you can go directly to the chapter on job search strategies. The same goes for all the chapters.

Not only is this book designed to give you a solid understanding of each topic but many of the chapters have questions and worksheets to help you achieve your goal. It is a workbook of sorts. I encourage you to fill in the blanks. In the chapter on interviewing, we even give you suggested answers as a guide. Then we give you the space to write out your answers. In the chapter, Keeping Track, there are forms such as: telephone log, activity log, pocket interview guide, networking forms and more. There is also a chapter devoted to effectively using the Internet.

They are designed to enhance your learning so you can be even more empowered and efficient in getting the job you want.

There is always work to be done in locating the right job. There are no shortcuts. This book, however, is designed to assist you in getting the job you want with as little work and time as possible. Congratulations! You've come to the right place.

2

COPING

THE WORLD OF STRESS

Welcome to the world of stress. Unemployment is dealing with potential financial woes and emotional swings. Emotions are difficult to measure. On the emotional scale, losing a job is near the top of the list, close to losing a spouse or a divorce. It is not fun nor is it something that you would wish on any friend.

Often the biggest battle with unemployment comes from within. For many of us, especially males, our jobs are a large part of our identity. If we no longer have a job, who are we anyway? It is no accident that the comment "What do you do?" is often the first question asked when getting acquainted with someone. Our identities are strongly associated with what we do.

I used to fish for fun.

Here is some good news. Finding a job is like fishing. You don't have to be a professional fisherman to catch fish. Anyone can land a fish; it just may take you a little longer. Likewise, you don't have to be a professional job developer to succeed in finding a new job. Even a first-time fisherman can catch a fish. Maybe not the biggest haul, but then who knows?

EMOTIONS, EMOTIONS!

After losing a job, there are a variety of ways that people respond to unemployment. Some people are elated, some are angry, some become silent and some fall apart. No one can predict what the reaction will be. Many times the outward expression is not the inward reality.

On the other hand, you may feel a need to vent. To release the inner hurts, frustrations, anger and disappointment can be a healthy outlet. Venting is a way of expressing your frustrating feelings at that very moment. Telling your most recent employer where to get off is probably not advisable. So venting can be beneficial or harmful, depending on where and how it is done. Acceptable places to vent might be any place where no one except a trusted friend or two might hear you. Places to consider might be at home or on a mountain hike.

Some people prefer writing or journaling. It is another acceptable way to vent. It is simply writing down your thoughts and frustrations in a private notebook or journal—not for other's to see. Venting can release some of the pressure that you feel inside. It does need to be recognized so writing or journaling can be used as a healthy outlet.

There are three primary emotions that take place. It may take some time but sooner or later, one or more of these emotions may become dominant. They are: depression, self-blame and withdrawal/isolation. They are not particularly "healthy" emotions if continued for any length of time. Awareness that these are temporary responses, often help individuals to cope.

SO YOU LOST YOUR JOB

There are many misconceptions regarding the unemployed. Those who act "OK" are often "NOT OK." They often are covering up painful emotions—sometimes even too painful to admit to themselves.

Another misconception is that the unemployed person thinks that most of their colleagues or friends who survived the RIF's (Reduction In Force) or cuts are relieved. While they may be relieved they were not cut, many of them suffer from survivor guilt and grief. They might be next? Those that were cut can be as good or better workers than themselves. There is a sense of unfairness. What do they say to an unemployed former coworker? There is often great turmoil in the company and they have to stay there and live with it. In dealing with cuts, RIF's and downsizing, there are SURVIVORS and VICTIMS. Which is which—we are often not sure.

"SO WHAT DO YOU DO?"

This can be a very painful question for many people who are unemployed. What does one say? First of all, they usually did not know that you are unemployed and meant no harm when they asked you this question. So what do you say? You can concentrate on your skills and profession and tell them you are in transition. Then you can ask them if they know of anyone in that profession. You can turn a potentially embarrassing situation into an opportunity to network. You can briefly tell them what you did and then ask them what they do. Remember, you have nothing to be sorry for. It was just an unfortunate set of circumstances that you were there at the wrong time.

TIME FRAME

So how long does it take to get another job? One week, one month, one year—no one really knows. Remember, it's just like fishing. How long did it take to get your first fish? The same principle applies here. Research shows that in the last few years average lengths of time are two-to-four months. But there are exceptions to this average. Is there a shortage or a surplus of eligible employees with your skills in the region, nationally? For some positions six months to a year is average. This unknown often adds to your personal stress.

IT'S YOUR CHOICE

Basically, you have two choices. You can become bitter, depressed or angry and nurse your wounds or you can take this "unfortunate situation" and use it as an opportunity to better yourself. This doesn't mean you're not in pain or that there may be some agony, depression, self-blame and withdrawal/isolation. In spite of all the odds, you have a choice. You can accept the situation and run with it or you can nurse your emotional wounds. While the choice may not be easy, it is ultimately yours. Most successful business owners have more often than not faced many failures and hardships along the way. They simply chose the better path. That doesn't mean it won't be painful. You can accept the pain but keep moving forward.

HOW'S THE FAMILY TAKING IT?

While coping emotionally, your family is an important factor. Whether or not your family members say anything, your unemployment has a significant impact on them—and not just financially. They know that you are stressed emotionally and may not be dealing very well with the situation. Sitting down with the family and being open and honest is often the best thing to do. This is particularly hard for males. To tell them your fears allows them to share their own apprehensions. Now you are in a position to help each other. Withholding your fears keeps you at a distance.

Let your family know your schedule. Research shows that between 25-35 hours/week looking for a job is often the most productive. Let them know what you are doing and why. At 35 hours/week, let's see, that would be 7 hours/day for the normal work week of Monday through Friday with your Saturday's and Sunday's off. That's probably less time than your old work schedule but remember, finding a job is often harder to do than the actual work day. So you need to keep you energy levels up. Once you've kept a realistic schedule for the day, stop! It's OK to stop and take a break. Treat yourself to the weekend. Give yourself a day off now and then. It often refreshes and works wonders. Remember, the exhaustion on Fridays when you were at a regular job. Give yourself the same break.

Allow for some time off. Use it as an opportunity to do some fun things with the family. Make plans that are low cost or free. It is not expected that you'll get an interview every day or every week, but you do need to build the framework so that it will happen. Finding some quiet time alone is also helpful. Use it to talk to your own soul and become refreshed. This can build energy and help focus.

If you have no office at home, create one. Use space in the bedroom or kitchen—any place that you can call yours, so no one will mess with it. You should plan your strategy and then keep good records (see Chapter 14—Keeping

Track). This will help you to keep track of your activity and give a sense of accomplishment.

BUT NOTHING'S HAPPENING

You may think nothing is happening but you are laying a foundation for a new future with solid plans and you are following through with hard work. It may not be fast enough but with a little patience it will come true.

Don't take rejection personally. I know this is easy to say but hard to do. Think about it this way. Most of the time when you end up on a "dead-end road," it is because there really is no job available and not because they do not like you. And most of your contacts have a difficult time saying there is nothing available. Think like them so you will not take it in the wrong spirit.

Form a support group. This can be a small group of 2-5 unemployed or recently unemployed people. Family members do not count—unless they have been or are currently unemployed. You need individuals who can relate to your feelings and personally know where you are emotionally. Set goals for yourself. This creates a lot of close ties and often gives you an emotional push. Meeting at least once a week works well.

Play the HMR game. So what is HMR? It is the "How Many Rejections" game. If you know absolutely for sure that at the ninth interview you would get a job, would you be discouraged at the fourth or sixth interview? You might be, but most people would know that in only five more interviews, you would land a job. It could actually be a motivator. How many interviews can you go through before you get depressed and discouraged? Even the best interviewers have only a one to four ratio. Remember, each interview is one step closer to that job.

Do you think and act like a winner? Do you think someone wants to hire you while you are depressed. It may be extremely difficult but if you act like a winner—you will be! Just focus on that.

Let's face it. Even though you think and act like a winner most of the time, there are exceptions. Especially, after that "perfect" job interview that looked so promising. So then, what do you do? Here are some suggestions.

- Spend some time in doing activities that affirm you

- Write out your fears, anger, depression, etc.

- Call or contact another unemployed person

- Compare your ups and downs to a regular job

- Let you feelings go, knowing that tomorrow you will likely feel better

THINGS TO KEEP YOU GOING

Exercise is a good anti-depressant. Find someone you like and exercise regularly with them. Join a club or get involved in some kind of team sports. Being part of a team will give you a sense of belonging which will benefit you during down times.

Take an inexpensive course or program. Any hobby or interest that you didn't have the time to do before but always wanted to do will be a great boost. Any of these activities should not be time consuming but can be a daily or weekly refreshment to your soul.

Get out of the house every day. Meet people for a cheap lunch or go window shopping. See other people. Don't be a hermit.

The "8—2 Rule." This rule will help guide you toward realistic goals. Do a minimum of 8 letters, 8 phone calls, 8 contacts, or 8 hours of work a day. Or, on the other end, no more than 2 interviews per day. Doing more than 2 interviews per day is too much. The emotional stress will show up in later interviews. Don't go to either extreme. Be realistic. Be balanced.

I always wished I could sleep in for a whole week.

DANGER SIGNS

Here are some signs that you may need help:

• Drinking alcohol abusively

• Suicidal thoughts

• Severe depression (remember: ups and downs are normal)

• Eating excessively or very little

• Major personality changes or mood swings

• Continuous thoughts of harming yourself or others

If any of these signs persist, please get some help from qualified professionals. Additional help can be found on the website: www.depression-screening.org. The diagnostic is free and also provides you with local professional resources for further screening and assistance. Assistance is readily available but you must make the first move. There is ample help even on a low or a no-cost basis.

FIVE COMMON MISUNDERSTANDINGS

Personal crises often create a spiritual earthquake. How does my spiritual life and this crisis relate? Since you have more idle time you may have been evaluating or reevaluating your spiritual life since you have become unemployed.

Often, some fundamental spiritual issues arise with unemployed people. They are frequently not expressed for fear that they would sound like they are blaming God. Others express it rather vocally, but that too may be a cover up. Some are too embarrassed or afraid to approach a friend, a professional or to even face it themselves but would welcome a dialogue with someone about what is troubling their souls.

There are five common misunderstanding people experience. You may experience all of them, some of them, or none at all. If any do apply, here is an opportunity to take a good hard look at what you really believe and why.

1. *"I must have done something wrong."*

This reason is an assumption of responsibility or guilt. Often deep-seated feelings of guilt (founded or unfounded) will be imprinted on our thinking. This can be harmful to emotional health if it is an automatic process.

There are good and legitimate reasons why one may be terminated. Perhaps this is a good time for personal evaluation. If there is a reason, deal with it in a positive way and go on from there.

There are also reasons beyond our control why we may have been terminated. Some examples are: poor company performance, company mergers, change in company products/strategy, downsizing and unreasonable bosses. If we take a careful and honest inventory of ourselves and it comes up negative, then it can be assumed that it was beyond our control and we should not assume guilt or blame. Many people may need help in working this process through.

2. *"I thought I did everything right! What happened?"*

For the person who was told "work hard, earn a good education and get a great job" and who did just that, losing a job can be devastating. What does all this say about education, hard work and dedication? Nothing really. The rules of the ball game have simply changed. Yes, what worked in previous generations may not work today. Today, there is no job security as we were taught. The unwritten but often honored rule of "you work hard for me and I'll take care of you" is gone forever! What was taught was true then, but now no longer valid. The old time-honored rules have changed. The shock of a job loss forces many people to come to grips with the new rules.

3. *"It must have happened for a reason."*

This misunderstanding assumes that there is another overriding factor why we were terminated. Management's explanation is only the mechanism since it is God's purpose that is being fulfilled.

To attribute the termination of one's employment to God gives a sense of "God is in control" and is very reassuring to many people. Others, however, may be using this as a cover or an excuse not to look more honestly and truthfully at their termination. This may be a good time to encourage them to look at other viewpoints as to how God works in their lives.

4. *"Is God punishing me?"*

You can take two approaches here. If you believe that God really is punishing you, don't you think you should find out why—if you don't already know? This is the first approach.

The second approach is: We may never know why this happened but believe that good can come out of all situations. Maybe God does not will evil on us but allows things to happen and then brings some good out of it. Often there is confusion about the will of God. This is a key concept that is often misunderstood and is well worth clarifying.

5. *"How do I know what God's will is for my life?"*

This is a hard question for most people to answer. There are, however, several principles that we can evaluate to answer this question. Here are a few sample questions that can get you started.

- Do I follow God's will or my own beliefs in what I know to be right and wrong?

- Do I seek God's guidance or meditate daily?

- Do I feed my spiritual or emotional life?

- Do I use the talents that God has given me?

- Does this job/career interfere with my family obligations?

- Do I enjoy this type of work environment?

I've read more books this month than in 20 years.

WHAT YOU CAN DO

If the issues mentioned above are real to you then you are encouraged to deal with them. Putting them off will not solve the dilemma nor will it help you. If you are unable to sort them out by yourself, perhaps a little extra help would be in order. Here are some suggestions:

- Obtain help within a religious setting, a support group, or close friends regarding your spiritual and emotional needs and understandings

- Read books about spiritual and emotional growth

- Seek out other unemployed people with similar views about life and obtain their help and opinions

- Seek help from qualified counselors, ministers or rabbis

You can use this as an opportunity to refine and improve your spiritual life. It may not come easy but the rewards are great.

3

ASSESSMENT TOOLS

You may already know what you want to do for your next job. Congratulations! You are part of a lucky minority. If this really depicts you then you can skip this chapter. However, most people are not really sure what they want. If they could just figure it out. It is a task well worth pursuing, but it often takes a longer time than you have to figure it out so you get another job—maybe it is not really to your liking, but then again it certainly puts bread on the table. If this describes you, the exercises below are designed to assist you in figuring out the direction you would ultimately want to go.

The first step to obtain rewarding work is to evaluate *yourself.* What are your values? What is it that you like doing? What are your skills and abilities? And lastly, is there a market for them? If there is a market, you like what you are doing and you are good at it, then you have a bright career future.

Many of us, however, need to take a closer look at ourselves. What are our values, skills and personal traits? Each of the following exercises is designed to assist you to focus and get a clearer profile of yourself. With this information, you can seek the jobs that will be more enjoyable and fulfilling.

VALUES

The purpose of this exercise is to help clarify what your values are and the role a job can take to fulfill them. Below are listed some values. Write beside each value how important it is to you. Write "H" for high, "M" for medium and "L" for low in importance. This is a partial but representative list. Please add, delete and redefine as you see fit.

_____ Achievement—accomplishing your goals
_____ Advancement—enhancing your ability to get desired jobs
_____ Authority/Power—being in charge

_____ Autonomy/Independence—designing your methods of achieving a desired
　　result
_____ Creativity—freedom to try your new ideas
_____ Recognition—praised for work well done
_____ Responsibility—being held accountable
_____ Security—job stability
_____ Social—fulfilling your social needs at work
_____ Service—contributing to some worthwhile cause
_____ Variety—frequent change of work
_____ Wealth—financially rewarding
_____ Other _____
_____ Other _____

Write below the top six of your high importance "H" values as they relate to a
career. If you don't have six, write the ones that you did label as High Importance
"H."

_____　　　_____
_____　　　_____
_____　　　_____

Questions to Ponder

1. To what degree were the values listed above fulfilled in your last job?
2. What type of work would you need to fulfill these values?
3. How much effort are you willing to put forth to fulfill them?
4. What questions could you ask in an interview that would help to determine
   whether or not that position would be meaningful?

TRANSFERABLE SKILLS

Many of the skills that we develop are transferable to our next job. Below is a lim-
ited but representative list of skills. First, check each ability you have and then
place a number next to each one checked. Rate your proficiency in that skill (scale
of 1-5: with "1" the lowest and "5" the highest.) See the example below.

	Skill	Proficiency		Skill	Proficiency
Example:					
Communication	✔	4			
Communication	___	___	Coordinating	___	___
Managing	___	___	Planning	___	___
Organizing	___	___	Analyzing	___	___
Negotiation	___	___	Editing	___	___
Interviewing	___	___	Leading	___	___
Listening	___	___	Motivating	___	___
Scheduling	___	___	Troubleshooting	___	___
Writing	___	___	Conceptualizing	___	___
Designing strategies	___	___	Computer skills	___	___
Research	___	___	Setting priorities	___	___
Implementing	___	___	Coaching	___	___
Training	___	___	Presenting	___	___
Recording	___	___	Controlling	___	___
Marketing	___	___	Advising	___	___
Other _____	___	___	Other _____	___	___

Take the top six skills that you marked (highest proficiency) and write them below. Next to each skill listed give an example of how you used each particular one.

SKILL	WHEN and HOW
Example:	
Conceptualizing	When a customer comes in with a complaint, I listen and ask a lot of questions if I don't understand.

Continued on next page.

1. _____

2. _____

3. _____

4. _____

5. _____

6. _____

Share the above information with a good friend to see whether they think it is a realistic list.

Below fill in the top six skills required for the kind of job that you are seeking? If you're not sure, you may need to do some investigating. Job ads (classifieds or Internet) are a good place to look.

1. _____   4. _____
2. _____   5. _____
3. _____   6. _____

Share this list with several people who are in this field to see whether they think that it is realistic.

Questions to Ponder

1. Has the list of your skills been revised since you asked your friends for their evaluation?

2. How does your list of personal skills compare with the job list you desire?

3. What skills need improvement?

4. How does all this fit in with your long-term goals?

ARE YOU STILL NOT SURE WHAT YOU WANT TO DO?

It could take a long time to figure out what you really want to do with your life—but in the meantime, you need a job to put bread on the table. Below is a list of questions that may take you some time to answer. Some answers may come quickly but more likely others will take quite a bit of thinking, pondering, sharing and discussing with those you love and trust. You might want to work through one or two at a time. Perhaps you can write them on a card to keep with you. Read it at a stop light or when you have a moment to yourself. Think about it, process it, then share your thoughts with caring friends and see what they think. There may be more than one "right" answer. Have fun!

1. Do I know what my *passion* is or is it just *intensity*? Is there a difference, a relationship?

2. In what ways can I measure the progress of becoming a b*etter me*? Is this external, internal, or both?

3. How do I know if I need to change from *within,* change jobs or both?

4. What are the essentials that make my life matter?

5. What ways can I make a deep connection with my *creative self?*

6. Am I being selfish when I reflect and ask "What should I be doing with my life?"

7. Should I wait and listen for my *calling* to appear or should I launch an earnest self-discovery process?

8. Is the thought "I must have a perfect dream job or nothing else" a way to procrastinate and live in a fantasy world?

9. What does career choice have to do with finding my identity?

10. What's more important for my focus: "What I **do** with my life or what will I **become**?"

11. Do I fear that a career choice is final and nonreversible?

12. Is it a mental trap to say "I'm keeping all my options open" and not make a decision?

13. Is having "so many talents and abilities," seem like a blessing or a curse?

14. Can I become blinded by "money, praise and/or opportunity" and lose sight of finding the *ideal* career?

15. When is "sacrificing for the family" a sell-out for not pursuing your passion?

16. In what ways can I overcome the fears of walking the *unknown path*?

17. How can I use failure as a path to success?

18. Solving most problems requires some guesswork and/or experimentation at best. So is it the same for figuring out the *right path* to follow in life?

19. How can I tell if my job search is motivated by avoiding the *negatives* of my present situation or the promise of a more *positive* future?

PONDERABLES

*Are these **true** or **false** for you?*

1. There are a few people who experience mystical insights. Most of us just hear a faint *whisper* that urges us to follow.

2. The path to a career we love may have many twists, turns and roundabouts.

3. A *jump start* to more meaningful work usually comes after a *personal crisis*.

4. *Embracing the dream* is more liberating than making lots of money now.

5. Working at a high income job for a time is rarely the way to fund your dream job.

6. *Doing the right thing* is hard since most of the time you *go it alone*.

7. I was created to live, work and dream *passionately*.

8. There is more than one type of work that I can love and still live *passionately!*

4

10 EASY STEPS TO A GREAT RESUME!

10 Steps to a Great Resume has been successfully proven hundreds of times. Very few people actually enjoy putting together a resume but our format is one of the easiest (at least less painful) to complete. Unfortunately, there are not short-cuts. Please follow the directions closely and you will be amply rewarded. To do it right will take you some time, but you will be proud of yourself when you finish. I know of no other "easy" way other than to pay someone to do it for you. Even then, there are difficulties.

Shortening my resume is like
cutting out half of me.

Not all of the sections need to be done in exact order. After #1 and #2 choose whatever order is most convenient for you. But keep in mind that it is to your advantage to go over all of the following sections to hammer home a polished and convincing resume. There is space for you to write your answers on the page.

1. **Job Objective**. Also called a job target, an actual job title works best. Here you must decide exactly what you are looking for, be it baker, candlestick maker or whatever. This will help you focus your thoughts so you will hit the target. If you're not sure what you want to do, then select a job title that you are interested in pursuing.

Example: Project Manager in the telecommunications or service industry

2. **Job Ad**. Write a typical job ad that matches your objective. (Include skills, abilities, knowledge, traits, education and experience, etc.). It probably is a good idea to go through the classified section of your local newspaper or on the Internet under job listings. Spend a little while reading the ads even though they may not be exactly what you are looking for. You can get a good sense of what to write down. Do you see anything in a particular ad, or maybe in a few of them that matches your personal abilities, etc?

Example: "Minimum five years in the telecommunications or service industry, interface closely with internal departments and external customers. Manage all phases of project life cycle including: development, execution, reporting and budgeting, etc."

Write down the job ad you would like to pursue. (Each bullet is for a qualification—minimum of 8)

- _____
- _____
- _____
- _____
- _____
- _____
- _____
- _____

3. **Summary** Statement. Match your qualifications for each of the items listed above in the job ad (#2).

Example: "Over 10 years project management experience in the telecommunications and service industries. Executed the entire life cycle of multiple projects including: development, implementing, reporting, budgeting and customer relations, etc."

List your qualifications for the job ad above.

- _____
- _____
- _____
- _____
- _____
- _____
- _____
- _____

4. **Summary Statement**. Use the information in the item above (#3) and write it out into the following format.

SUMMARY STATEMENT

A professional with over_____ **years** *(don't go over 20)* **of experience in the** _____**industry.**

Experience/expertise includes: _____,
_____, _____,
_____, _____,
_____, _____,
_____, _____,
_____ **and** _____,
A person who is *(personal traits: self-starting, aggressive, knowledgeable, experienced, deadline oriented, motivated, able to multi-task, etc.)*
_____, _____,
_____, _____,
_____, _____,
and _____.

(Optional) **Has a** _____*(Security clearance, key certifi-cation, etc.)*

5. **Accomplishments**. For each key qualification (include skills, abilities, knowledge, traits, etc.) listed above (#4), think of several accomplishments from your past work history to illustrate that particular skill or qualification.

1st Example: "Developed an operational analysis model."

2nd Example: "Good customer relations."

- _____
- _____
- _____
- _____
- _____
- _____
- _____
- _____

6. **Accomplishment Statement**. Describe each accomplishment *(listed above in #5)* in a simple, powerful, action statement that emphasizes the results that bene-fited your employer. The more effective statements follow this format: (a) verb/action, (b) to what and (c) the result. *(See the sample **Action Verbs** list below for suggestions)*

1st Example: "(a-verb/action) Developed (b-to what) an operational analysis model (c-result) which resulted in a more efficient budget analysis."

2nd Example: (a-verb/action) Initiated (b-what) a progress review schedule for the customer (c-result) which enhanced their involvement and satisfaction."

- _____
- _____
- _____
- _____

Continued on next page.

- _____
- _____
- _____

ACTION VERBS

On a resume you usually begin each job responsibility or accomplishment sentence with a verb. Below is a list to help get you started.

Accomplished	Edited	Managed
Activated	Effected	Manipulated
Advised	Enlarged	Marketed
Adapted	Established	Modified
Adjusted	Evaluated	Monitored
Administered	Examined	Motivated
Adopted	Executed	Negotiated
Advertised	Expanded	Obtained
Analyzed	Expedited	Organized
Arranged	Explained	Persuaded
Assembled	Facilitated	Prepared
Assisted	Fabricated	Presided
Built	Familiarized	Presented
Calculated	Formulated	Programmed
Cataloged	Fostered	Processed
Chaired	Generated	Promoted
Changed	Governed	Proposed
Collaborated	Guided	Publicized
Compiled	Hired	Recommended
Completed	Identified	Recorded
Conciliated	Illustrated	Recruited

Conducted	Implemented	Related
Contracted	Improved	Revised
Constructed	Increased	Specified
Consulted	Indexed	Synthesized
Coordinated	Indoctrinated	Surveyed
Created	Influenced	Sorted
Defined	Informed	Supervised
Delegated	Initiated	Stimulated
Demonstrated	Innovated	Studied
Designed	Integrated	Taught
Devised	Interviewed	Uncovered
Directed	Invented	Used
Distributed	Investigated	Wrote
Drafted	Maintained	

7. Make a list of the **primary jobs** that you have held. Do this in chronological order (beginning with your most recent) for the past 10-15 years. Include any unpaid/part-time work that fills a gap or that shows you have the skills for the job. Some of your personal qualifications would be very helpful.

Example: NOW Telecommunications, Inc.   "1993-2001"

Project Manager

1ˢᵗ

_____, _____, _____   _____
Company   City   State   Dates

_____
Title

_____
Description *(List only 5 or 6 activities/tasks that would help qualify you for your next job)*

_____

_____

_____

Continued on next page

2nd

_____, _____, _____   _____
Company   City   State   Dates
_____
Title

Description (List only 5 or 6 activities/tasks that would help qualify you for your next job)

_____

_____

_____

_____

3rd

_____, _____, _____   _____
Company   City   State   Dates
_____
Title

Description (List only 5 or 6 activities/tasks that would help qualify you for your next job)

_____

_____

_____

_____

4th

_____, _____, _____   _____
Company   City   State   Dates
_____
Title

Description (List only 5 or 6 activities/tasks that would help qualify you for your next job)

_____

_____

_____

_____

8. **Education** and **Training**. Make a list of your education and training that is related to the new job that you want. This also includes "on the job" training.

Examples: B.S.—Electronic Engineering, University of Delaware
Certificates—Project Management, Harper Institute

_____

Degree   *Major*   *Institution*   *City*   *State*   *Date (Optional)*

_____

Degree   *Major*   *Institution*   *City*   *State*   *Date (Optional)*

Degree   Major   Institution   City   State   Date (Optional)

Certificate   Type

9. **Community Groups**, **Associations**, **Volunteer**, **Languages,** etc. (Optional)

Example: Volunteer—Boy's Club of America (Local #372).

---

10. On the next page is the most popular format. It is called a chronological format, since it is listed by work dates in order. Now, put all the information from
the proceeding pages into the chronological format which is listed below. If you
have worked hard to make the information above complete, you will now have a
good and convincing resume. (See sample resume on page 31.)

CHRONOLOGICAL RESUME FORMAT

Page__1

Name _____

Street Address _____

City, State, Zip _____

Phone(s) _____

E-mail _____

OBJECTIVE _____

_____

SUMMARY _____

_____

_____

_____

_____

_____

_____

_____

_____

_____

_____

_____

_____

_____

NOTE--You may want to make several copies of this sheet (one for each placed worked).

Name _____   Page _____

EMPLOYMENT HISTORY (most recent first)

_____   _____
Employer, City, State   *Date(s)*

_____   (_____ yrs)
Job Title   *If more than one title*

Responsibility Statement

_____

_____

_____

_____

_____

_____

Accomplishments

- _____

  _____

- _____

  _____

- _____

  _____

Name _____   Page_____

EDUCATION (Degree, major, school, city, state, *date--optional (skip* high school if you have any college).

_____

_____

_____

_____

_____

OPTIONAL HEADINGS—Professional Development, Associations, Community Groups, Languages, Volunteer, Military Service, etc.

SAMPLE RESUME

Here is what a sample one page resume would look like when you have finished our easy steps.
A two page format is also acceptable.

ROOSEVELT PATEL
1665 Ruthland St. • Carlisle, PA 17225
(515) 555-2279 • rpatel@verizon.net

OBJECTIVE
Project Manager in the telecommunications or service industry.

SUMMARY

A professional with over 10 years experience as a project manager in the telecommunications and service industries. Experience includes: the complete project life cycle (development, execution, reporting, budgeting, etc.), interfacing with management and customers, servicing a broad scope of industries (aerospace, telecommunications, automotive, healthcare, chemicals, etc.) Superb organizational, motivational and team building skills. Excellent time management and computer skills (database, spreadsheet, accounting and word-processing). Certificate in project management.

EXPERIENCE

NOW Telecommunications, Inc., Carlisle, PA   1993-Present
Project Manager
Managed the Open Solutions Terminal Testing program. Supervised 17, wrote business programs and processes, led cross-discipline teams.
- Designed an efficiency program which showed a 9% increase in efficiency per year.
- Increased production by eliminating unnecessary procedures and reducing turn-around time.

Gateway Data Services, Inc., Camp Hill, PA   1991-1993
Product Manager
Directed product marketing and pre-sales activities. Determined product content and technical direction. Supervised a staff of 12.
- Executed a strategic marketing plan which created $1.6 million in sales the first year.
- Configured demonstration system resulting in a compelling product demonstration.

EDUCATION/TRAINING

B.S.—Electrical Engineering, University of Delaware

Certificates: *Program Management,* Harper Institute
                 Excellence in Customer Service, Bart Business Development, Troy, Michigan

COMMUNITY

Coach–Boy's Club of America (#372)

COVER LETTER

The function of a cover letter is to add a little clout with a personal touch that will give you an advantage over another person applying for the same job.

GENERAL INFORMATION: Your cover letter should include the following features.

- Make it individualized

- It should tailor your unique background to the job

- Demonstrate that you have done your homework

- Explain any glaring problems in your resume—gaps in work, etc.

- Suggest the areas in which your skills fit

- Address to a specific individual—*not* "To Whom It May Concern" or "Dear Sir/Madam." If you don't know the individual, "Dear Hiring Manager," "Dear Professional," or "Greetings" are acceptable

- The first line in the body should identify the position for which you are applying

- Follow an acceptable business letter format

- Physically balance it on the sheet

- It is not to be a summary of your resume

- A cover letter should accompany each resume sent out. When sending your resume via the Internet, the cover letter is the "body" of the email and your resume should be an "attachment," unless otherwise stated.

CONTENTS:

Opening paragraph

- States the particular job category or title that you are seeking and how you found out about it.

Center paragraph

- Relates your specific experience or educational accomplishments that would help you qualify for the position.

- Expand the emphasis of any special skills or explanations that you have.

- Demonstrates that you know something about the company.

Closing paragraph

- Explains the easiest way that the prospective employer can get a hold of you.

- Asks for an interview.

SAMPLE COVER LETTER

Roosevelt Patel
1665 Ruthland St.
Carlisle, PA 17225
(515) 555-2279
rpatel@verizon.net

October 21, 2004

Hiring Manager
Summerville ViaNet, Inc.
P.O. Box 713
Harrisburg, PA 17356

Dear Hiring Manager,

I am responding to your advertisement in the *Harrisburg Tribune* of October 17 regarding the position of *Project Manager.* Attached is my resume for your consideration.

I have worked in the telecommunications industry for many years. I think that I have much to offer. Not only do I enjoy my work, but I am always looking to improve and learn new skills. I saved my previous employer over $705,000 last year. I hope that I am the type of candidate that you are looking for.

I can be reached at (515) 555-2279 during the day. Looking forward to hearing from you.

Thank you for your consideration.

Sincerely,

Roosevelt Patel

enclosure

REFERENCES

It is also very helpful to have a list of references ready to submit. Generally, you wait for a request for your references and do *not* send them with the cover letter and resume. References confirm to the prospective employer that you are honest and responsible since you are willing to share the opinions of others about yourself. There are several acceptable formats that can used, but the following information should be taken into consideration.

- **Professional references**: Former colleagues (associates, bosses and people you have supervised) that can speak about your character and quality of work.

- **Character references**: To attest to your honesty, attitudes, outlook on life, loyalty, etc.

- There should be a minimum of 3 references, but 5 to 6 are preferred. They may ask for only 2 or 3 but this way provides a backup in case someone is ill, traveling or cannot be reached.

- The best people who can attest to your skills, abilities and traits are coworkers, supervisors and associates. Neighbors and long-time friends are acceptable for personal references (maximum of 2).

- Use a variety of people with different backgrounds and generally do not use all the references from the same place. Avoid the use of pastors, rabbis and priests since it will identify your religion.

- No relatives are to be used!

- Choose only people who will promptly reply. by mail or easily reached during the day. Avoid people with the same last name (surname) as yours.

- Ask them ahead of time if they will be willing to be a reference. Also, ask if they have a preference whether to list a home number or a work number. Some people don't like to be interrupted at work and others at home.

- As with the resume and cover letter, the reference list must be typed. Make it neat and as perfect as your resume and cover letter in a matching type style and paper.

- In addition to name, address, phone number and email, add your relationship to them and for how long. *Example:* Coworker—3 years.

SAMPLE REFERENCES

References for
ROOSEVELT PATEL
1665 Ruthland St. • Carlisle, PA 17225
717-555-2279 • rpatel@verizon.net

John Abernathy
7865 H Street
Gettysburg, PA 17325
717-555-4407
Colleague—8 years
NOW Telecommunications, Inc.

Susan Johnson
215 Jessop Rd.
Camp Hill, PA 17655
717-555-9985
Team member—3 years
Gateway Data Services, Inc.

Jennifer Tate
6654 Tulip Lane
Harrisburg, PA 17699
717-555-7854
Director—2 years
Gateway Data Systems, Inc.

Michael King
8694 Lake Blvd.
Holly Springs, PA 17355
717-555-8327
Neighbor—6 years
Community leader

Clifton Cady
7843 Bonifant Rd.
Harrisburg, PA 17699
717-555-4572
Colleague—4 years
NOW Telecommunications, Inc.

Mark Spring
45668 Oak Hill Rd.
Gettysburg, PA 17325
717-555-2238
His supervisor—3 years
Gateway Data Systems, Inc.

All the above are home addresses and phone numbers.

5

JOB SEARCH STRATEGIES

PRODUCTIVITY

The productivity of your job search depends on several factors. As you worked through the exercises in the self-assessment section you probably saw several things that you could do. In order to do the best job search, you need to narrow the field down to two or three specific job categories to do a quality job search. When you look at fields too broad, the possibilities seem limitless and you can feel overwhelmed and lose focus.

There are several considerations, which can help target your job development. Some considerations are: location, type of company, size of company and job market openings (present and future projections).

Once you have narrowed your choices to a workable size you should do some targeted or specific research on the companies out there. People who use this strategy are often amazed at the number of companies. There is an abundance of library books and Internet resources. A good place to start is with Chapter 6—Surfing the Internet.

MARKETING STRATEGY

There are three broad methods of doing job development—traditional methods, networking and the Internet. Traditional methods and networking are discussed at length in this chapter. An entire chapter is devoted to the Internet (Chapter 6—Surfing the Internet).

Traditional Methods

Classified Ads

The traditional methods of job development include: classified ads, job agencies and search firms. The classified ads are perhaps the first place that one thinks about when looking for a job. However, only about 15% of jobs are acquired by this method. While there are usually real jobs listed (some are fictitious), there is also an over abundance of people seeking jobs by this method. It is estimated that even though most of the jobs advertised are real over half of them already have someone selected for the post. They are simply following policy to advertise all job openings or they think that it is a good political strategy to advertise. That way, when someone

internally asks why they selected such and such a person they can say that they advertised for the most qualified person. Whether that is really true or not is very hard to prove or disprove. A typical ad can attract 100-300 resumes, so you can see that your competition is extremely intense. Also, many of the traditional classified ads from newspapers are now solely on the Internet.

Job Agencies

Job agencies are another resource for employment that is often overlooked. Agencies are growing rapidly because more and more companies are relying on them as a primary source for most of their employment needs. Agencies used to provide employees chiefly for clerical, office support and manufacturing, but have more recently expanded into many other areas such as mid-level management and some executive jobs. Jobs from $15K to $50K have been the traditional base for agencies but now they have moved up the income ladder and often reach $100K. Just check any major city newspaper and you'll see. Job agencies can be divided into three broad categories—permanent, temporary and temp-to-perm. Temporary and permanent work have existed for a long time and is well understood but temp-to-perm is a relatively new category. Many companies including large corporations now hire only through agencies on a temp-to-perm basis. Temp-to-perm is a method where your first 3-6 months are considered "temporary" but plans already exist to potentially make it permanent. At the end of the "temp" phase, provided there is still a need and you're doing an acceptable job, you're converted to a permanent position. This is often called a buy-out. Nothing has changed—just your status. Your paycheck will now come directly from the company, not the employment agency. Vacation time, health benefits and retirement benefits usually begin at this time.

Agencies with "temp-to-perm" status are used more and more by companies that like to "try out" their new employee for a few months to see if they are a good fit. So don't be misled by the title "temporary." Most of the "temp-to-perm" employees get asked to stay on full-time. This also gives you an opportunity to *try out* the company. Either party can break the agreement without any adverse consequences.

Search Firms

There are two types of search firms—retainer and contingent. The retained firm usually has a contract with the companies that they serve for a year or more. This is renewable and so there is a vested interest to serve the needs of the company. Under this contract the firm receives a regular monthly fee. If there are no openings to fill or if they have several openings that month, it doesn't make any difference. In other words, if the company estimated that there would be 12 positions that need to be filled in the next year and the average income for each position was $100K, they would pay the retained agency $30-35K per month (typical fee)—regardless of how many positions they were trying to fill in that particular month.

A contingent agency gets paid only if their candidate gets hired. It is similar to the traditional real estate agent. Make the sale—get paid. No sale—no pay! Traditionally, the contingent agents are in the lower income bracket ($50-$100K), but there are always exceptions.

A good source to find search firms is in the *Directory of Executive Search Firms*. It is in most libraries and is updated each year. There are places on the Internet but many of them charge a fee. Just go to any search engine such as *Yahoo* or *Google* and key in "executive search firms."

Most firms specialize, so it is important that you contact those agencies that service your specific field of interest.

It is recommended that you use several search firms or job agencies because not every firm or agency services all the particular companies with which you may be seeking employment. I call them "One A Day Multiple Agencies." I think five is a good number to work with.

A word of caution. Companies do not like your resume to come from multiple sources. If this happens, many companies will not consider you a candidate. A way to control this is to not allow any agency or search firm to send your resume to any potential employer without your permission. This way you can keep track of who gets your resume.

Many job hunters let search firms and agencies take the lead. They go home and wait for the agency to call. This is not considered the most effective method. Agencies and search firms look for candidates that show initiative. "What can I do over the next few weeks to make myself more qualified?" is a question that you should ask the agency. Whatever they recommend, if anything, you should seriously consider. They are the professionals and generally good at finding employment. On the other hand, you can also ask "What can I expect of you over the next several weeks?" This question indicates you are serious about placement. Try to get something measurable—number of phone calls, number of hours, etc. Follow up in a week or two. If they don't seem to be doing their part, don't cut the bridge, but spend most of your energy on other agencies.

Don't get stung by an agency that requires a fee from you. An agency with a good reputation does not do this. In total, agencies fill about 5%-10% of open positions.

NETWORKING

Networking is very effective but also time consuming. Approximately 60-70% of all jobs are filled by this method. It might work quickly but most likely it will take some nurturing. Because it is so effective, I recommend that over 50% of your job search time should be spent networking.

There are many ways of networking. Networking can have positive or negative connotations depending on your experience. Many people think that networking is asking for a job from someone you know or from a friend's friend. Got that? Networking is basically utilizing your own friends to gain information that will lead to a job. At it's worst it is begging for a job but at it's best it is exchanging information and interests so that all parties could benefit. Done properly, it is a win-win proposition.

Unemployment is taking a course:
"How to Find A Job."

When you are looking for work, most of your friends and neighbors don't know it unless you tell them and that is where networking comes into play. It is hard for someone to give you leads, ideas or encouragement if they don't know that you are searching. So, the first thing to do, is to get the word out—that you're looking for a job.

So who do you tell? Anyone that knows you! It's that simple. You can ask for information from people who may know something about your targeted job market. Remember, most people use this method to get a job.

Often when there is an opening a company will first advertise it internally. Frequently, people in the company have a friend or an acquaintance who can fill the vacancy so he will tell them about it. This has been a very effective way for a company to fill openings, even a large corporation. Most people in a company are more than willing to assist you by letting you know about the position, but first they need to know that you are looking. This is why you need to let as many people know that you are job hunting. Remember, no one can help you if they don't know you are looking!

It is important to know that, it is a two way street. You need to be genuinely interested in the company as well. How can you help it? Well, you need to talk to people to find out. Maybe it's some information regarding a hobby or a sale on an item they are looking for. Maybe it's some technical thing about a computer or some knowledge you have about cars or service stations. It can be anything that they need—and we all have needs. Since you are not working full-time, you just might be able to fit "whatever it is" into your schedule.

You can start with your friends, neighbors, relatives, classmates, church members, former work friends and others. This may work well. However, you may need to go beyond that level. There may not be any openings where they are currently employed but tomorrow may be another story. People don't know if that is the case and neither do you. Develop a good reputation with them and then when there is an opening—bingo, someone thinks of you. If you did not get to know or assist anyone when they needed help, why would they think of you? Remember, no one knows when or where most job openings are going to occur. The secret is to be visible and competent, so when there is a job opening, you will be there at the right place and at the right time.

This does not happen by chance but by strategic planning on your part. Just think, when you are employed, you can keep on using this method.

Another effective way to network is through professional organizations. If you don't know of any group, just ask around. There are usually several to choose from. Any given group can be a rich source of information and ideas. I don't mean that you should just join any organization, pay your dues and do nothing more. Once you've joined one, show up regularly at meetings—meet and greet, show your face and get acquainted with as many members as you can.

Become visible! "How can that be done?" you ask. There are many ways but here are a few to consider. Become a volunteer. Volunteer to pass out materials (assuming there are some) for a speaker at a meeting. Volunteer to write an article or two for a newsletter. Visibility—remember! Offer to help when there is a call for volunteers. One word of caution. Volunteer only for tasks that will bring you visibility. That is important. That way you both win. They get a task done and you get visibility!

Another way to network and build relationships in a professional setting is to get to know the members in a more meaningful way. Just knowing them by name or as acquaintances isn't very effective.

So how do you get to know people on a deeper level? Not by asking for something from them, that's for sure! Why not ask individual questions regarding their business or career? Look for ways to be helpful and offer them help. This is not a time to ask people for ideas to get a job or job leads. You need to build trust and a relationship. You don't accomplish that by asking for things to benefit yourself. However, you may request a business card in order to keep them in mind and to refer anyone who might use their services.

I wouldn't offer people my card unless they asked. Often they do ask, but not always. Now that you have their card, write down on the back the date and event where you met. You might want to email a thank you in a few days for chatting and that you haven't forgotten to refer people to them. Stay in touch. Building relationships—that's what networking is all about. It works, it's effective and more people succeed with this method than any other. So, when are you going to start?

6

SURFING THE INTERNET

Below is a rich source of Internet sites to help with your job search. Since there are so many different ways to use the Internet, they are divided into easy-to-understand sections. Even though it is a widely used method less than 10% of all job searchers find work this way. We therefore recommend that you limit searching on the net to no more than 25% or your time. Spend the rest of your time using other methods—especially networking.

META OR MULTIPLE SITE SEARCH

These sites are not your usual job listing sites. They are faster and more powerful because they search over 300 different Internet job sites at once. When you find the job you are interested in, click on it and it links you to the better known Internet sites (like www.careerbuilder.com or www.monster.com) that lists the particular job. This is a very effective way to look at hundreds of sites all at once, saving a lot of time and energy. Besides, it lists job sites that you may not be familiar with.

www.employment911.com
www.alljobsearch.com
www.jobsniper.com
www.grassisgreener.com ($11.95/3 mo.)

GENERAL OR JOB BANKS

Some of the most popular sites are listed below. They list all types of jobs throughout the entire USA. Sometimes they include Canada. You can limit your search to the geographic area desired.

www.ajb.org
www.careerbuilder.com
www.jobs.com
www.career.com
www.hotjobs.com
www.careersite.com
www.careermag.com
www.employmentguide.com
www.monster.com
www.nationjob.com
www.careercity.com
www.jumboclassifieds.com
www.jobbankusa.com
www.net-temps.com
www.direct-jobs.com
www.thingamajob.com
www.careers.wsj.com
www.directemployers.com
www.firstgov.com   (federal government jobs)
www.usajobs.opm.gov   (federal government jobs)
www.fedworld.gov   (federal government jobs)
www.fedjobs.com   (federal government jobs)
wwwfederaljobsearch.com   (federal government jobs)

SPECIALTY JOB BANKS

Specialty job banks are sites that list work in specific occupations or industries. There are sites just for accountants, bankers, salesmen, computer workers, nurses, teachers, insurance people, electricians, manufacturing workers, engineers and many others. Since there are so many, it is difficult to list them all but the "link" sites listed below link you to specific specialty sites that you might be looking for. Below the "link" sites is a sample list of specialty sites for computer jobs.

Links to Specialty Sites

www.jobhuntersbible.com
www.interbiznet.com
www.quintcareers.com
www.itsyourjobnow.com   (go to "Nitch Network")
www.worktree.com
www.jobsearchsites.org
www.job-hunt.org

Computer Specialty Sites

www.computerjobs.com
www.computerwork.com
www.dice.com
www.softwarejobs.com
www.techies.com

EMPLOYMENT AGENCIES

Employment agencies fall into two categories. They are: the traditional job agencies (full or part-time) and executive search firms. (See Chapter 5—Job Search Strategies.) They also have many good jobs. Listed below are some national agencies—both traditional and executive. Don't forget to check with your local and regional employment agencies. Many of them do an excellent job. Internet yellow pages or your local yellow pages directory are also excellent resources.

National Employment Agencies

www.olsten.com
www.spherion.com
www.adecco.com
www.ajilon.com
www.ajilonfinance.com
www.manpower.com

Executive Search Firms (Head Hunters)

www.searchfirm.com
www.bluesteps.com   ($129/yr)
www.executiverecruiter.com
www.ipa.com
www.headhunter.net
www.ekornferry.com

ASSESSMENTS

For people who are not sure what type of job they should pursue, the sites listed below are an excellent source for assessment tools. Some sites charge for their assessment tools but many do not. The first site listed (www.quintcareers....) gives an excellent overview of many sites on the Internet. It also tells you whether it is free or pay and supplies an evaluation.

www.quintcareers.com/online_ assessment_review.html (assessments list)
http://online.onetcenter.org
www.typefocus.com
www.kingdomality.com   (8 questions—humorous)
www.jvis.com/   (289 questions—$14.95)
www.assessment.com
www.workzone.net

WORK AT HOME DIRECTORIES/ RESOURCES

These sites assist you in finding work that you can do at home. If you are interested in working for yourself, these sites are great.

www.careersfromhome.com
www.workathome.com
www.bizoffice.com
www.gohome.com
www.homeworkers.com
www.youcanworkfromanywhere.com
www.freeagent.com
www.guru.com
www.mysteryshopper.com
www.shadowshopper.com

RESEARCH—INDUSTRY/COMPANY

For researching a specific company or an industry, these sites are excellent. It always pays to know a little about a company when you network or go for an interview.

www.vault.com
www.brassring.com
www.wetfeet.com
www.hoovers.com
www.newsdirectory.com   (industry trade publications)

COMPANY LOCATIONS

You can search by industry, a specific company or an occupation. Searching company sites has proven to be the most time effective way to locate a new job. While we don't encourage you to limit your search to just company sites, it is a wise investment in time and energy even if it seems slow and you don't find too many appropriate jobs. Because it is a slower process many people search other popular ways (www.monster.com, etc.) and that is what makes going to company sites first so effective. You have a lot less competition. Also, many companies list their job openings on their site first and only post on general sites if they haven't received enough qualified candidates.

www.careersearch.com
www.acinet.org
www.hoovers.com
www.yp.net
www.switchboard.com

ASSOCIATION LISTS

Many companies belong to professional associations. Below is an assorted list of sites that you can search by different industries or occupations. Most professional organizations list their member companies. They often list job openings for the respective companies as well.

www.asaenet.org
www.businesstown.com
www.ipl.org:2000/div/aon/
www.weddles.com/associations/index.htm
www.recruitersnetwork.com/resources/associations.htm

MISCELLANEOUS

This list of various websites is tailored for specific needs. Don't forget to also look at local, state and county government, schools, hospitals and other institutional sites. They often have their own web site that lists job openings.

www.careeronestop.org	(lists state employment centers plus other sources)
www.clearedconnections.com	(jobs that require secret or top secret security clearances)
www.bwni.com	(business women's network)
www.bizjournals.com	(lists top 50 or 100 companies, agencies, etc. in specific cities)
www.certcities.com	(an exhaustive list of computer certifications)
www.eop.com/	(jobs for the disabled)
www.earnworks.com	(jobs for the disabled)

www.greentogray.com	(from military to civilian careers)
www.salaryexpert.com	(occupational salaries)
www.salary.com	(occupational salaries)
www.acinet.org	(look under "Wages and Trends")
www.vistaprint.com	(free business cards)
www.depression-screening.org	(free depression check-up)

7

JOB FAIRS

Job fairs or career fairs as they are sometimes called are additional outlets for you to get some exposure, sell yourself and hopefully find that "perfect" job. A job fair is a marketing event for both parties. You are marketing yourself as a job candidate and a company is marketing itself as a good place to work. It is a way for companies to gather resumes and interview candidates for positions currently open or that will be open sometime in the future.

There are generally three types of job fairs:

1. Commercial sites—planned by others. These are often in hotels, motels and stadiums.

2. Company sites—usually on the company premises looking for good candidates.

3. Outplacement companies—produced on behalf of a company that is downsizing some employees.

The success rate for job fairs is very low but it doesn't have to be that way with you. Your basic goal is to make a good impression. And it is usually the small things that can make a difference. Most candidates come, hand out resumes, do some talking and leave—never to hear from a company again. There is a better way. View job fairs as a beginning point for establishing a relationship. More on that shortly.

GETTING PREPARED

You need to be properly dressed and groomed just as if you were going to a regular interview. After all, they will be interviewing you. Maybe not as lengthy as a formal interview but dress and image is just as important. Have multiple copies of your resume along with your references and any portfolio that would be appro-

51

priate. As with any interview, an extra pen, licenses, certifications and your "information/generic job application" sheet should be your companions. It is not out of the ordinary for them to ask you to fill out a job application, so be prepared. Remember, your goal is to make a good impression.

When they say, *"Tell me a little about yourself"* it is a good idea to have a "one minute marketing speech" ready to go. It is a 60 second (or less) talk where you tell them four things about yourself.

They are: Who you **are**
             What you **do**
             What you **want**
             What you **can do for them**

Here is a sample response for a project manager position.

"I am a project manager specializing in software development for the logistics industry."

"I take a project through its entire life-cycle from conception to completion."

"I'm seeking a similar position where

I can use my well-earned reputation of completing tasks under budget and on-time."

Get the idea?

Now write one for yourself incorporating these four ideas.

_____

*Who you **are***

_____

*What you **do***

_____

*What you **want***

_____

*What you **can do for them***

Two other questions are commonly asked. They are: *"What kind of job/position are you looking for?"* and *"Do you have a current resume that I could have?"* Please, never say "any job." You may think that it shows flexibility but it seldom comes across that way. They usually think you're desperate or really don't know what you want. Either conclusion does not help. As to resumes, of course you're ready with a copy!

ASKING QUESTIONS

One of the best ways to show interest is to ask questions. Ask a lot of questions. Don't read them from a written list but have them in your head. Below is a great list to get you started.

"What actually does this job involve?"
"What critical skill sets are you looking for?"
"How do you see me or someone filling your needs?"
"How many employees do you have doing this kind of work?"
"What positions do you anticipate or currently have open?"
"Can you tell me a little about your company?"
"Realistically, what are my chances?"
"Do you have a business card that I could have?"
"When can I expect to hear from you?"
"If I don't hear from you within the next two weeks, may I call or email you?"

THE FOLLOW-UP

Going to a job fair should be just a beginning. You should walk away with several different business cards. Then, send an email to thank people for talking with you. In about two weeks email them again or call up to check on your status. No pushy sales talk—just a question to see if you're still being considered. Then, if you don't hear from them in a week or two, email or call again just to let them know that you are still interested just in case someone else has *not* been offered the job. If they have asked another person, who has accepted, email or snail mail them a "thank you" note for being considered and wish them well.

If you are still interested in a future opportunity with the company, email them once every three or four months just to touch base. All things being equal, you'll make a much greater impression for the next opportunity.

8

INTERVIEWING SECRETS THAT WORK!

For over fifteen years I have coached people to be effective in an interview and have developed effective methods to obtain gainful employment. I want to share two secrets. Anyone can master the art of interviewing. To some people it comes naturally, to others it doesn't—but everyone can do it. To conquer your fears and go confidently to an interview, you need to know these secrets.

TWO MAJOR SECRETS

Knowledge

Knowledge is the first secret. Know the kind of questions that are going to be asked and learn the types of answers the interviewers desire. Knowledge consists of what to say, what *not* to say and when to say the proper things. Knowledge of the kind of questions to ask and *not* to ask is also important. I will guide you with suggested answers later in this chapter. Are you thinking that all this information is difficult to master? Well, it really isn't.

Another part of *knowledge* is to know your skills. What are your strongest or most marketable skills? Could you rapidly list three or four? Would the skills mentioned be vague or would they match specific aspects of the position that you are seeking? Once you left, would you think of *other* skills that would be more appropriate to mention?

It is important to practice not only what you will say but how you're going to present yourself. One suggestion is to smile; not a stiff and continuing grin but an occasional smile. Don't look stupid, but be calm, assured and appropriate. Even if you are not sure what to say, smile a lot and believe that you will succeed—then you will succeed. You may not get a job offer from that interview but you most assuredly will at a future interview. A few rejections should not change your attitude and drive. If you go with great expectations, you'll be off to a good start.

Practice

Practice is the second secret. I would suggest that you practice interviewing to build up your confidence. You may want to get together with one or two other people who could give you some reasonable feedback. None of us is perfect and if you would like to ace the interview, surely you would like someone to give you an honest evaluation.

Pay attention to:
- appearance
- eye contact
- composure
- mannerisms
- poise
- quality of answers
- communication ability
- enthusiasm
- motivation

Pay special attention to motivation and enthusiasm. I'll tell you why later in the chapter.

Rate yourself. Better yet, have your friends rate you on each of the criteria *(from above)* for each answer and not just one overall rating for the mock interview.

Even better, use an audio or video cassette. Go back, listen to your words, your intonation and the way you present yourself. Go through and correct your mistakes. Then go back and practice again and again, until it is smooth, short, concise and convincing. Keep asking yourself better ways to present yourself and answer questions. Practice makes perfect. Generally, your answers should be no longer than 30-45 seconds per question.

If you had the authority to interview and hire, would you hire the person on that audio or video tape? Be really honest (you want that job don't you?): and keep practicing until you can say a definite YES!

So there you have it—**knowledge** and **practice!** They are the major secrets of a successful interview. It almost seems too simple to be true. I have watched people go from failure to success because they used these two secrets. I've also seen people repeatedly fail because they didn't think that these key factors are important. It is not complex but it will take some time to learn the techniques—yes, a good amount of time, but the results are rewarding. It's like swimming. Although the basic techniques are simple to learn, you must practice a lot to become good. If you want a job badly enough, you will take the time to learn them! So why not take the plunge?

Interviewing need not be terrifying. Most people do *not* like interviewing and I am no exception. Most of us are scared because we don't know what we'll say when we are asked certain questions. We're afraid of giving an embarrassing answer. We get nervous, our nervousness shows and we often do the very things we fear the most. As you continue, you will begin to understand the magic of interviewing and, of course, overcome your fears and concerns.

It is important to remember that the interviewers are just as human as we are. Some of them do excellent work, some of them do poorly, but most of them are somewhere in between.

PREPARATION FOR THE INTERVIEW

In addition to practicing a mock interview, preparation involves three additional items:

(1) researching the company
(2) visiting the site
(3) knowing what to bring with you

In some cases, it may not be possible to research each company but often there is much you can do. Chapter 6—Surfing the Internet is an excellent place to start. Another method of research is to ask for a copy of the job description of the position for which you will be interviewed. This means will better prepare you. It will also impress the interviewers, since it shows that you are serious about working for them.

The second thing to do is to visit the site before the interview. When you go for an interview, you're excited and want to make a good impression. The main reason for a pre-visit is to reduce your anxiety. The route becomes familiar and you won't waste any emotional energy finding your way there. Secondly, it gives you a travel time frame. If it takes you a half hour, give yourself an additional thirty minutes. Here's why—Perhaps there is more traffic than usual or there is an accident which can cause a delay. So allow yourself a little more time. You can avoid feeling rushed or anxious. If you get there early, you can go over your interview questions in your car or the lobby.

Thirdly, knowing what to bring with you is important. So when you are actually called, you can go through the checklist. (See *Pocket Interview Checklist* in Chapter 14—Keeping Track.)

Remember these points for the interview:

- *Bring extra copies of your resume.*

  I've been amazed at how many interviewers can't find their copy of your resume or who have lent it to somebody who hasn't returned it. They will often ask: *"Do you happen to have an extra copy of your resume with you?"* And if you don't, they will be embarrassed and so will you. They often ask questions regarding items on your resume. It is more professional simply to pull out one for yourself and/or for them.

- *Bring a copy of your references.*

  References are often requested during an interview. Remember, your reference page should match the type face, formatting and paper style of your resume.

- *Bring a couple of extra pens.*

  As fate would have it, when you bring only one, it will run out of ink or won't write. It also looks unprofessional to ask for a pen to fill out paperwork. Blue or black are the only acceptable colors, but black is probably better.

- *Information sheet/another job application.*

  This information sheet consists of all the past employers, employment dates, addresses and brief job description, etc. Or you can bring any filled-out job application form. Then you can transfer the information to the company's application form. Only a very few people can remember all the details, such as: street numbers, phone numbers, zip codes, etc. Instead of asking to use the company phone or to get back with the interviewers regarding the information, impress them with your efficiency and "can-do" actions.

- *Dress and grooming.*

  Clean—that is the word! Clothes, body, hair, shoes, etc. No need for detailed explanations but there are too many people who don't bother to do the simplest things to come out a winner at an interview. If you are going to drive, how about a clean and neat car? I know human resource/personnel people who actually walk you to your car so they can see whether it's tidy and clean. It's an indicator of your personal habits.

- *Bring light reading material.*

  A magazine or something easy to read is acceptable. Newspapers are not good, but more details shortly.

- *Garlic, onions and other good stuff!*

  Many of our favorite foods and condiments make for great eating but not before a job interview. So watch those foods that are known for their pungent odors since they can turn off many people.

YOUR ARRIVAL

Always arrive early! Go to a restroom and check your appearance: hair, clothes, etc. Look in the mirror and do a 360° turnaround. Look for loose threads, lint, dandruff, dirt marks, etc. Avoid an embarrassing moment. Use any other facilities in the restroom that will free you to concentrate on the interview. I once went to a job interview that lasted three and a half hours. Fortunately, I was prepared.

Calming exercises can help. Deep breathing and stretching exercises can also help you relax. Hey, doing this stuff on a long-term basis could also calm you down for your entire life. Do anything (within reason) that you know will help. Maybe giving yourself a pep talk would be very helpful. Review any of the questions that you think need a memory jog. Lastly, pop a breath mint, but don't chew gum.

OUTER OFFICE

First impressions count the most. It is just as important to establish a good initial working relationship with the receptionist or secretary as it is to do so with the people interviewing you. Often, an interviewer will check with the employee in the outer office to get their impression of you. This could include your attitude and composure as well as your words. On occasion, receptionists or secretaries will give the interviewer their impression of you without any prompting. Typically, this happens if they are uncommonly impressed with you—either positively or negatively. So, mind your manners!

Often you will be asked to fill out some forms, such as a job application, a writing sample or a profile sheet. Any writing that you do is part of the impression that you will give. How neat and complete is it? For most, printing is better than script. Do *not* write: *"See resume"* on any job descriptions and do *not* leave anything blank. If it does not apply write down N/A (not applicable) or put a line through it. This way your interviewer knows you saw the question rather than having overlooked it. In the "job description" section, list first those things that would be applicable to the job under consideration. Then go down the list in descending order of potential importance. Be specific and brief. If the application asks for a job title and there wasn't one, just use a descriptive word or two. Hiring managers will often, be looking at your job application before your resume.

Explain any gaps in your work history. A federal government personnel employee once told me that if there was any unexplained gap three months or longer, the assumption would be that the person had been in jail. A strong negative assumption to be sure, so please give an explanation. There are numerous valid reasons why there might be gaps in your work experience. Also, any required signatures take on legal implications, so read carefully before signing anything, including the job application.

While you wait, you might want to look at a magazine. It is not a good idea to read a newspaper. The reasons are simple—turning the pages is disruptive, noisy and newsprint ink that gets on your hands could also get on your clothes or any forms you may need to fill out. Whatever you read, just make it light, nothing heavy or detailed. Save your energy for the interview!

THE INTERVIEW

Be genuine and don't entertain the interviewer. This is not the time for you to put on a show or any type of comedy routine. How much talking vs. listening should take place? Research indicates that it is best to let the interviewer talk 50% to 75% of the total time. There will be times, I'm sure, that you will do more talking but listening is important. I remember an interview at which the interviewer insisted on talking about 85% of the session. I was initially uncomfortable but decided that it was his style, so I relaxed and nodded my head a lot. It went much better and I was offered a follow-up interview. So the ratios are not a hard and fast rule but a good general one. The key is not to dominate the conversation. We like to talk about ourselves and when someone is listening, we sometimes tend to go on and on thinking we are making a good impression—this is not so. So make your sentences short and to the point. In general, most answers should not go beyond 30-45 seconds. If the interviewer wants to know more, you will be asked.

When interviewing, we often emphasize our qualifications. Since most positions have a variety of qualifications, what should we emphasize? Obviously, the qualifications important to the job. So how do you know what they are? One way is by simply asking, *"What are the two or three most important qualifications for this job?"* or *"If you were to prioritize the qualifications for this position, what would be at the top of that list?"* Then you will know what is important to the interviewers. It is no longer a guessing game. Maybe it is getting along with colleagues, maybe it is meeting deadlines, etc. Give this matter close thought. Then you can direct your answers toward what is important to them. This should be done fairly early in the interview. You don't have to wait to ask this kind of question. You'll be surprised at some of their answers.

QUESTIONS, QUESTIONS AND MORE QUESTIONS!

How many questions should you ask? There is no magical number, but it should be quite a few. First, not asking questions may indicate your lack of interest. I have observed cases in which the overall interview went very well—up to this point. Then when asked: *"Do you have any questions for me?"* the job seeker would say: *"No."* This response left a very poor impression.

Remember, interviewing is a two-way street. The interviewer wants a qualified person who can get along well but also wants you to be satisfied. Otherwise, you will not stay long and the process will have to start over again—not a cost effective situation.

The question: *"May I ask about the wages and benefits?"* needs to be handled cautiously. In most cases, put it off for as long as possible. The reason is very simple—you don't want to look like one of your primary interests. Wait until the end. Better yet, wait until they bring it up. The longer time you have to *sell* yourself, the greater the chance that you will be getting a better deal. So don't rush it. Remember, the more you seem to fit the company's needs, with your qualifications and personality, the more likely you are to get a good offer.

Sometimes, the interviewer will bring up the question of salary early in an interview. Put it off as along as possible. There is little benefit in negotiating at the onset.

Never criticize your former employer. It doesn't make any difference whether a boss fired you or you hated him. Avoid this kind of talk, but if and when the question of why you left your former job comes up you can always say that you didn't always agree. That is very different from criticizing the former company. If the interviewer presses the issue, it is better to take most of the blame regardless of what happened. You could say there was a personality conflict and simply move on. Remember, what you say about your former employer is more a reflection upon you than upon him. Once a person who was interviewed asked: *"What type of people generally work here?"* The interviewer answered by asking a question: *"What type of people worked where you were last employed?"* When the answer was: *"Oh, they were a bunch of really hard-nosed grumpy people,"* the interviewer responded: *"That's the kind of people you'd be likely to find here too."* Enough said!

I GET SO NERVOUS

Many people are very nervous during an interview. I once viewed a video tape intended for interviewers; not for interviewees. The presenter asked over 100 human resource people, personnel directors and other hiring managers to write down the three things they liked the most and three things they liked the least about their jobs. Then he asked them the question: *"How many of you put interviewing as the top three preferred things?"* Three or four hands went up. Then he asked: *"How many of you put interviewing in the bottom or least liked?"* Nearly all the rest responded. This was enlightening. Interviewers dislike interviewing as much as interviewees do! In fact estimates reveal that only three to five percent of all interviewers have any formal training. Most of them learn on the job—and some not too well.

This gives us hope. Now you know you are probably not the only nervous person at an interview. Not only that, you could do something to help relax the interviewer. Just think, it might win you some goodwill. A good way to do this is to generate small talk about the interviewer. Remember, people like to talk about themselves. But use judgment here: don't stray far and long from the business at hand.

TELL ME A LITTLE ABOUT YOURSELF

This is the question that often begins a formal interview. The interviewers do not want to know anything about your past except whatever relates to the position. So here's your chance to make a real sales pitch. Don't take too long to answer the question (30-45 seconds) and do so in an orderly fashion. Focus the content on your skills, professional growth and dreams and how they relate to the potential new job. Practice answering this question. First things said have the greatest impact and are the longest remembered. Put a little passion into it. Remember, if it's a boring to you, it's probably boring to them.

GET AWAY FROM YOUR RESUME!

Interviewers will ask you about your resume for two reasons. First: They want to know whether it reflects you. Does it represent you? Second: they want to know more about specific items on it. Talk about it, fill in the gaps, flesh it out more.

They may review several items, ask you questions, verify information and/or request additional information. Some interviewers, however, will use your resume as a crutch or as an outline for the interview. That may make us feel good because it will suggest that they are looking us over carefully. But while some review of the resume is necessary, your resume should not be the major focus of conversation. I know this sounds crazy but remember that the interviewers are hiring someone to solve problems. And if you ask about their problems, their challenges, tasks, headaches, you create a much greater impact. People are quick to talk about themselves and their qualifications but few concentrate on their problem-solving abilities—especially with regard to those challenges at hand. One easy way of accomplishing this is ask how they see your skills or abilities would fit into the job.

A next logical step might be to ask for a typical challenge, problem or issue that is related to the position. Ask how the candidate for the position can help and assist them with the typical challenges. By asking questions and probing, you are demonstrating your interest in problem solving.

In a sense, you are simulating an on-the-job situation as if an employee would go to the boss for help and guidance in order to resolve an issue. Remember, people like talking about themselves and their problems. You are talking with your interviewers about their "work" problems. Some typical questions might be:

"What challenges does this job have?"
"What are the headaches of this job?"
"How does this job interrelate with other departments?"
"What are the potential friction points?
"How do you propose to solve them?"
"What role do you see the new employee as a problem solver of these issues?"

Then, listen to the suggested ways that you could support them in regards to these matters.

What you are doing is taking a subtle lead. You are not dominating or controlling the conversation but nudging its direction. You are leading simply by asking questions and letting your interviewer do the talking. It may take you five seconds to ask the question and they may take a minute to answer. Who is leading? You are! Who is talking the most? He is! Subconsciously you are perceived as the problem solver. You asked for typical problems but then listened for the possible solutions. You are not going to get hired for having all the answers. You are going to be hired because you are willing to work as a team member in order to explore and find solutions.

Listening is a powerful tool. It shows interest, attention and concern. To most people it is interpreted that you care and that is a powerful message you want to convey.

STORY TIME

Tell relevant stories. People remember stories more easily than abstract information. Personnel directors often say that after a long day of interviewing: *"Everything is running together. I can't remember who said what, but I do remember the stories or illustrations they gave."* So when there is a: *"Tell me about…or give me an illustration when…"* from the interviewer, it is your chance to tell your stories. Have three or four of them ready so you will be prepared for each kind of question without stalling for time.

Stories should have three elements:
   (a) a situation or issue
   (b) your action
   (c) the outcome

Make sure they contain positive outcomes and exhibit your skills!

EXAMPLE:

Question: *"Tell me about a time when you went above and beyond your regular job duties?"*

Answer: *"Once I saw that the (a) boss was bogged down with instructing different workers about different jobs (b) so I volunteered to help train some of them on the in-house software. (c) The training was successfully accomplished and the boss appreciated my volunteering."*

The above example showed the (a) situation, (b) your action and (c) a positive outcome.

See if you can think of one, or maybe a couple of situations.

EMOTIONS WIN OVER LOGIC

One key element to selling yourself is this: to remember that most people make their decisions on the basis of *emotion* rather than by an objective analysis. You have already been pre-approved when they looked at your resume—before they even saw you. It is important to keep in mind that emotional impressions are crucial in decision making. Research shows that people with inferior resumes get hired if the interviewer feels good about them even though they are not as qualified. If you are as qualified as the others just remember this: if they like you they will hire you and if they do *not* like you they will not hire you—no matter how qualified you are!

One of the major goals in an interview is to make people like you. You must be honest about this. It can be done in many ways, but more about that shortly. Remember, most people make their decisions as a response to emotions or feelings and then support their feelings by logic. If they say: *"I would like to hire so-and-so"* and their boss asks why, they don't want to say: *"I just kind of liked him."* They will give some objective answer so that their boss thinks they have some logical or rational reason for the recommendation. Understand the process?

ILLEGAL AND INAPPROPRIATE QUESTIONS

Illegal and inappropriate questions focus on race, age, religion, national origin, sex and marital status. If your interviewer asks you: *"Are you married?" "Do you have any children?"* or *"What religious affiliation are you?"* they have stepped over the line. There are a couple of things to remember. Your interviewer may not know that these questions are illegal. Even if they know they're illegal questions, they may ask one or two anyway just to evaluate your response. You may not know their motives but be careful how you answer.

Here are some suggestions.

* Do not be offensive or defensive.

    There *is* a neutral ground.

* Respond to what you think is the motive for asking the question.

    Example: If an interviewer asks *"Do you have children?"* there may be a concern about the number of sick days that you might take. A good answer would be: *"If you are concerned about attendance, let me assure you that my attendance record is excellent."*

* Volunteering private information too quickly may jeopardize your employment chances.

    Example: If you are asked, *"Are you married?"* you may not care to answer directly. But there may be an ulterior motive for asking the question. They may want a married person or they may not and you most likely don't know the real motive. So simply asking a question like *"I'm just curious how marriage status fits into the job, could you help me out?"* might be a good answer.

BALANCE QUESTIONS

Balance questions need to be answered carefully. They are questions designed to trick you on either extreme. A typical balance question is: *"Would you be willing to put in overtime?"* An eagerness to work overtime might indicate that you socialize during the day and then make it up at night, thus getting time and a half for your work. On the other hand, if you're not available to work some overtime, you might come across as too rigid. A good answer might be: *"I'd be willing to work overtime at a seasonal rush or if someone is out sick."* Balance is the key. Don't make extreme answers.

Another balance question might be: *"What would you do if you saw a fellow employee repeatedly using the company telephone for personal long distance calls?"* An answer like: *"I would report it immediately"* would make you a tattletale. On the other hand, if you answer: *"I'd probably ignore it,"* you may seem lacking in loyalty to the company and the work. An appropriately balanced answer might be: *"After I had observed repeated violations I would take him aside and tell him of the consequences to the last guy who did it. Beyond that I probably would not do anything."*

An additional balance question is: *"How anxious are you for a promotion?"* Either extreme is not wise. If you're not interested in growth and promotions, you may not be highly motivated. At the other extreme, too great an eagerness for a promotion may indicate a lack of interest in the work on its own terms. An acceptable answer might be: *"My first goal would be to learn and do this job well. Then, if you're interested in using me in some other capacity, I'd certainly be glad to consider it."* Remember, use balance!

NEAR THE END

At the end of the interview, there is a tendency to summarize your skills, abilities and qualifications. It would not hurt to briefly recap a qualification or two, but to make it a major emphasis is wasting time. Most interviewers are going to make up their minds on an emotional level. So what do you do? Simply emphasize how much you enjoy (emotion) doing that kind of work. That will reach the emotions of your interviewers. What can you say? Try this:

"This is the kind of job that I look forward to do."
"This excites me!"
"I could really get into this!"

I WANT THIS JOB

Should you come right out and ask for the job? There is a lot of discussion regarding this question in the placement industry. Some experts encourage people simply to ask for the job. *"I know I can do this job, will you hire me?"* Others say that this method is too bold. So what should you do? Be as assertive as you can without feeling uncomfortable. If you are not comfortable, it will show. Maybe you can't describe exactly how, but the interviewer will sense your discomfort and it will work against you.

THE EXIT QUESTION

At the end of an interview you may ask the question: *"When can I expect to hear from you?"* Often the response will be: *"In a week or two."* Then you can say: *"If I don't hear from you at that time may I call or email you to find out about my status?"* Many people left an interview who thought they did very well but are not contacted after a reasonable time regarding a job offer. This can cause self-doubt and misgivings. Some think of things that they should have said or not have said. Often, they read too much into the silence. With the second question you made for yourself an escape route from all those frustrating *"What ifs…"*

9

INTERVIEWING—Great Answers for Tough Questions

Listed below is a set of questions that are commonly asked at interviews. Remember, short answers are better. Thirty to forty-five seconds are sufficient for the typical answer. If an interviewer wants longer answers, you will ask you; but you will generally not be stopped if you are giving longer answers—enough to harm you. Any question about your job history, resume and job application is fair game. Listed below there are questions with short but representative answers. Use them as guides. Space is also provided for you to write your answers. Make your answers honest. Don't make up stories. Try to remember things about your experiences that show your best side.

You may want to write out answers for all of these questions and then practice orally with a friend to answer them. Yes, it will take you several hours of work but before you groan too much please answer this question: *"Do you want to be prepared for an interview, or after you fouled up a few questions at an interview then WISH you had been prepared?"* Need I say more?

For the questions that ask for a situation or an experience, write down two possible situations or experiences for each one. Interviewers may ask you for more than one example for the same question but they seldom ask more than two. And don't forget these steps:

(a) situation or issue
(b) your action
(c) the outcome

1. Why should I hire you?

Identify your skills, dreams and character in relation to the job at hand.
Example: "Over the last several years I have sharpened my project management

skills. I enjoy this kind of work. It motivates me to continue learning and increase my skills. That way we will both win!"

2. Tell me a little about yourself.

Describe your job history, again stressing your skills, dreams and character traits; always relate them to the job that you are seeking.
Example: "I am a professional project manager with a bachelor's degree and hold a project management certification. I have always enjoyed organizing and motivating people to get a job done. Ever since I was elected sports' activity director in high school I saw myself in a leadership role. I would like very much to put these skills to work for you."

3. Tell me about the most difficult task that you faced at your last job.

Remember the formula: situation, action and outcome.
Example: "Once, one of my team members came to me and was quite upset at a comment my boss had made. Immediately after he left, my boss came in and insisted on knowing about our conversation. I wanted to be loyal to the company and at the same time be trusted with confidence by my team members. I told my boss that what was said was said in confidence but I assured him that I was not doing it at the expense of the company or of him. My boss didn't like it at the moment but several weeks later said that he respected me for my integrity."

4. How did you learn about our organization/company?

Response varies. Add a little information to make it positive—not just neutral.
Example: "I initially saw an ad on the Internet. Then I found a quarterly financial

report. Recently I met someone who works in the billing department. I am impressed with the continuous growth that your company has experienced."

5. Other than the required abilities, what skills do you possess that could enhance this position?

Do your research and be specific.
Example: "In addition to feeling very competent in the project manager role, I enjoy marketing which could be used in assisting the market department when they show perspective clients the actual project. I also believe that I have strong negotiation skills."

6. Tell me about a specific area of responsibility that you have enjoyed.

Relate it to the potential job.
Example: "The specifications for my last project were inadequate. I take pride that I caught the problem spots, carried out the research necessary to correct them and completed the project on time."

7. What have you been criticized for in the past two years?

Be honest but show how you improve from experience.
Example: "If the entire team is overloaded, I sometimes take on too much work for myself rather than delegating it. I'm getting better, but I can still improve."

8. Describe your ideal and least ideal boss.

Describe the ideal and then say that the least favorite type would be one who doesn't meet the standards you've defined. Stay positive.
Example: "The ideal boss trusts me after I've proved myself and so I am not micro-managed. I work better that way. My least favorite type of boss would not come up to those standards."

9. When you are confronted with an unprecedented decision, what do you do?

Have several examples ready.
Example: "Seek counsel and advice from others. Try not to make a rash decision. One time, over half of my team was out sick with the flu. I knew the project would not meet the date we'd agreed on for completion, so I went to my supervisor, who renegotiated a completion date and approved some overtime pay. The firm rarely granted overtime. It worked out in the end."

10. How do you criticize subordinates?

You should make it clear that you do so in private, with sensitivity and a lot of encouragement.
Example: "I remember once when I needed to talk seriously with a team member who frequently came late. I took him aside and asked him what were the reasons for his lateness. Before making any decision I always try to hear from the employee who is in trouble. We were then able to work it out successfully."

11. How important were communication and interaction with others in your last job?

If the true answer is "very much," say so and give an example.
Example: "A lot! One time when I was having each team member give an update, one employee questioned a technical decision another person had made. It turned out that he was right. We corrected the situation and it saved us many thousands of dollars."

12. When, given the option in a professional setting, were you a follower or a leader of a team?

Response varies. Give an example.
Example: "I volunteered for a team lead role at my last job. I think that I'm a good follower but I really enjoy leading a team."

13. Tell me about an accomplishment that made you proud.

Make yourself look good!
Example: "At my suggestion, I was assigned to reevaluate the entire process for approving projects. Several steps were combined and some eliminated. It took several months but once we got the bugs out, the new system worked extremely well."

14. What makes you feel successful?

Center on success related to work and give only three or four ideas.
Example: "When I make a customer happy, I feel successful. I remember once when I showed a customer a better technique for configuring his database. It saved him over three thousand dollars per year."

15. What motivates you to improve and progress in your career?

Limit to three or four items.
Example: "I like challenges, but to see a well-functioning company that is constantly striving to improve brings out the best in me."

16. Tell me about a time when you went beyond the call of duty.

Use the formula: situation, action and outcome.
Example: "Once when I was a project manager, I lost three team members during the final stages because of an auto accident. I worked sixteen-hour days with the team so we could get the project finished on time. We were successful."

17. Would you rather design/develop plans and procedures or implement/manage them?

Be honest.
Example: "Actually, I enjoy doing both but since I've been a project manager for some time, I now feel more comfortable with implementing and managing."

18. What would your supervisors need to do to get the best out of you?

Give three or four good actions.
Example: "Show me what needs to be done, make sure that I have the necessary tools, tell me that they believe in me and then let me go on my own. That really motivates me!"

19. Have you had to make or implement an unpopular policy or decision?

Explain. Make the outcome positive.
Example: "I remember once when I collected the time cards for the week. The new policy was that if employees were late, then the pay for the week would be put into next week's paycheck. I had to enforce it several times at first and with unhappy employees, but after a few months everyone concerned said the plan worked much better than the old procedure."

20. What professional situations cause you to feel awkward?

Limit it to one—and be brief.
Example: "When upper management required me to tell my subordinates, who had done nothing wrong, that they have been terminated due to downsizing."

21. What are your professional goals for the next three to five years?

Demonstrate a desire for growth.
Example: "I would like to get some more training and certifications. That would make me more valuable to an employer and myself."

22. What is your overall impression of your current or last employer?

Stay positive!
Example: "Most of the time we got along really well. Sometimes we would have a difference of opinion but we always seemed to work it out. I had a lot of respect for him."

23. Give me an example of a crisis situation at work that involved you.

Use the formula: situation, action and positive outcome.
Example: "Once my boss complained of chest pains. He didn't want us to call 911 but we did anyway. Later, we found out that he had a heart attack and we probably saved his life."

24. Tell me about a time when you were angry in the workplace.

Remember: situation, action and positive outcome.
Example: "Once my supervisor renegotiated a new and tighter deadline with the customer without consulting me. I felt that it left insufficient time for completion. Because the project wasn't completed by the new deadline, I lost my bonus. After a thorough review, the firm acknowledged that the deadline had been unreasonable and reinstated my bonus."

25. Has there been a time when another person's anger was misdirected at you? What did you do?

Be fair and show maturity.
Example: "Once an associate accused me of stealing money from his wallet. I was upset but didn't say anything except deny the claim. Later he found the money and came back to apologize. It paid off to stay cool under pressure."

26. If I were to offer you this position, how would you spend your first two weeks?

Listen a lot, ask questions and prepare for the work.
Example: "Listen, observe, ask lots of questions and learn as fast as I can."

27. Can you define integrity for me?

Keep it related to work.
Example: "To treat people with the same respect and honesty as I'd like to be treated while always performing my optimal best in the workplace."

28. How would you respond if a team member was taking too many breaks?

A balance question (see page 66—Balance Questions).
Example: "I'd probably ignore it at first, but if it is was repeated too often, I would probably call him aside, remind him of company policy and point out what happened to the last person who continued to take excessive breaks. I hope that that would resolve the problem."

29. If the company were to give you $3,000 as a bonus, how would you spend it?

The answer will show your values, so make sure you don't give a flippant response.
Example: "I'd probably put some in savings, pay off a little more on the car and go out for dinner."

30. What interests, related to the workplace, do you have outside the office?

Think of activities that demand your work skills and will benefit the company..
Example: "I coach a baseball team that my colleagues have organized for our children."

31. How do you establish working relationships with people?

Listen, ask questions, show interest.
Example: "I've learned that I can discover a lot about people if I just listen. Sometimes it's about work and sometimes it's personal. For anyone who is shy, I might at first ask some work related questions. That's safer territory."

32. Give me three adjectives that others would use to describe you.

Make these answers positive and relate them to work.
Example: "Others might say, 'Quiet, hardworking and professional.' I'm not really sure."

INTERVIEW QUESTIONS IN REVERSE!

Interviewing is a two-way street. You need to ask questions to help evaluate the job and make a good decision. This also shows that you have an interest in the position. Don't be afraid to ask questions.

You may use a cheat sheet, but don't pull out a long laundry list to review before selecting the questions you want to ask. Or better yet, memorize the questions ahead of time but don't sound too mechanical. With these questions and their answers you may want to provide a follow-up comment. This will reinforce the impression that you are a good candidate.

1. Why is this position open?

Company: "It was created just now to fill a gap in our new operations."
Your follow-up comment: "I know that this will be a challenging position and I feel sure that I am up to it."

2. What would you like done differently by the incoming person?

Company: "To pay more attention to detail."
Your follow-up comment: "I trust that I can be that kind of person."

3. How would you describe your management style?

Company: "I don't like checking up on people every hour. I give an assignment and then expect the workers to follow through. Of course, if they have questions, I'd expect them to come to me."
Your follow-up comment: "That suits me just fine!"

4. What do you consider to be your most important objectives for this job?

Company: "To be able to develop reliable estimates of cost and time."
Your follow-up comment: "With a little practice, I should become efficient at that."

5. How do you measure success?

Company: "To be able to grow and learn a little each day."
Your follow-up comment: "I've always liked to improve and see whether I can do a better job each time."

6. What freedom would I have to determine my work objectives, deadlines and methods of measurement?

Company: "Not too much at first, but as you learn the job we'll give you more."
Your follow-up comment: "I'd like that; I like proving myself."

7. Could you tell me about some of the larger challenges of this position?

Company: "To be able to handle the extra work that will be expected as the company grows. At some point, we'll have to get another part-time person."
Your follow-up comment: "Well, I'm up to a challenge, but I'm sure you'll be fair if I get overwhelmed."

8. Are there any significant changes planned in the immediate future?

Company: "Yes, one of the managers is having surgery and will be out for about two months. We'll need to share a lot of overtime."
Your follow-up comment: "I'd be glad to do anything I can to help."

THANK-YOU NOTES

Are they effective? Research shows that the effectiveness of thank-you notes may be marginal, but not always. The sooner the interviewer receives it, however, the better the impact, if any. How soon? Why not send it out the very day of the interview? In fact, why not take a small formal "thank you" card with you to the interview? Fill it out in the lobby or in your car and after the interview mail it at the closest mail box. They'll get it in one or two days.

More people (in spite of word processing and emails) still prefer a simple, attractive and handwritten personalized thank-you note. What do you say? *"I appreciate your time and would like to have an opportunity to do this kind of work."* Another idea: *"Thank you for considering me for this kind of work. I really would enjoy it."* A simple and not overly emotional but considerate response is the key. Don't review your qualifications. That got you the interview. Now the company is concerned about a good fit and feeling comfortable with the selection—YOU!

So there you have it! These time-tested methods and ideas can be put to good use. Go ahead and dream about the words: "Congratulations! You're hired!" It will become a reality!

10

NEGOTIATING WITH EASE

Negotiating can be fun! Some may feel anxious about negotiation but it doesn't have to be that way. Negotiating is an art as well as a skill. If basic principles are followed, they can safely lead you to a happy ending. With a little information and some practice you can become confident with any negotiations.

The first principle of negotiation is to show respect and fairness. This is not a time for rigidity or a demanding attitude. You must be willing to trust, respect and compromise. Think of it as a win-win proposition.

Know your worth before you negotiate. If you don't, you may accept a salary that you will later regret. There is no magic formula to determine you're worth. Market value, their bottom line and your experience and skills are some of the variables. However, you can get some idea of the going rate for your skills, education and experience. There are many web sites (*See* Chapter 6—Surfing the Internet) and other sources to help. The *Occupational Outlook Handbook* of the U.S Labor Department (which can be found in most libraries and on the Internet) and professional associations are excellent sources. They usually provide salary ranges. So plug in your information and determine what is a fair range for your services.

Different sources offer different data and methods of analysis. You need to compare and develop a range that you think is fair. The bottom of this range should be close to what you will accept as a minimum. For example: if a project manager in your industry makes a salary from $50K to $80K then your range should be somewhere above $50K and near $80K. It might be $65K to $80K.

WHAT IS YOUR SALARY REQUIREMENT?

When asked this question, it is better not to give your salary or salary range at this time. Let me explain. It is generally advisable to try and learn their salary or salary range first. It is said "He who speaks first loses" in negotiation. Keep that in mind! Here are some suggestions to handle this.

"I'm more interested in doing _____ at your company than the initial offer. What did you have in mind?"

"I will be glad to consider any offer that's reasonable and fair which I know you'll be. What did you have in mind?"

"I could give a range but based on your salary scale where do you see me fitting in?"

You turned the tables on the interviewers by asking the very question that they would have asked you. Your goal is to get them to give an amount or salary range *first!*

If they decline, then you will need to give your amount or a range. A range is generally a safer way to go. Use a little vagueness to your advantage. For example, you could say *"I was looking for something between the mid-60's to the upper 70's. How does that sound to you?"* Always ask for feedback after you've given something. It helps you know their thoughts and where they're coming from.

A "back and forth" strategy will help you reach common ground, that is equal to or above your minimum salary—what you decided *before* the interview. This shows that both sides are willing to compromise. Congratulations if you reach an agreement by this method.

If the negotiations are stalled or frozen at a several thousand dollar gap, then alternative options need to be engaged. Negotiating is an art. There is no *one way!* As long as both sides desire the services of the other there is hope. When one approach doesn't work, then try another angle.

Understand the variables such as budget constraints, salary ceilings and executive mandates. Figure out what those variables might be and make alternative suggestions to solve or work around them. Negotiation is offering a proposed solution to the problem. If one proposed solution doesn't work, say "I understand your concern" and then try another. If they don't accept that solution then come up with another one. You need to have many possible solutions ready to go.

Get the idea? Below are several scenarios to clarify this tactic. Some may be appropriate in your case, some may not.

- "I am *especially* interested in this job but I'm not sure I can lower my salary requirement. Could I have 48 hours to think about it?" (Usually they'll call before the 48 hours and make another offer.)

- "I'm curious. Do you have an educational fund? I was planning to take some courses to further my education. I would be glad to substitute the $4,000 difference in our salary negotiations with a written commitment to help cover my educational expenses up to $4,000. How does that sound?"

- "Since we seem to be close, would you consider a six month review (instead of the annual review) with measurable outcomes? As long as I measure up then you could give me a raise at that time. How does that sound?"

- "I have six months of health benefits left in my severance package. Would you consider delaying my health benefits for six months and putting the difference in my salary?"

- "I've been accustomed to four weeks vacation. I know that you can't extend your two week policy for new employees but in exchange for the salary difference would you consider a two week leave of absence without pay as a compromise. That way I get four weeks (time off), you don't break your two week vacation policy and we will be able to compromise on the salary. Is that workable?"

- "Is this your final offer or is there still room for negotiation?"

There are hundreds of trade-offs, compromises and deals that can be negotiated. You are the one who needs to have several alternatives to bring to the table. Remember, as long as they are talking, there is hope.

WHAT CAN YOU NEGOTIATE?

Negotiations can cover anything but here are some typical topics relating to salary and benefit negotiations.

Sign-on bonus
Vacation
Health
Insurance
Club memberships

Trade association fees
Telecommuting
Computer or laptop
Parking fees
Travel expenses
Stock options
Education/tuition
Time off/leave of absence
Clothing allowance
Convention expenses

Larger corporations tend to be more rigid but there is some bargaining room if you are a good negotiator.

WHAT ABOUT EMPLOYMENT CONTRACTS?

Employment contracts are becoming more prevalent but represent a rather small segment of the job market. These contracts are generally for sales, upper management and people who are in the *know* about company secrets. They usually include:

• Length of guaranteed employment

• Under what terms you can be terminated

• What kind of severance you can expect if you are terminated. (Sometimes known as the "golden parachute")

• Restrictions of future employment

If a company doesn't normally give contracts for the position that you are seeking, it is unlikely that they would accommodate this request. On the other hand, if they do, you would be wise to find out the general industry guidelines regarding the particulars for the position.

SIGNING THE DEAL

Whether it is in contract form or not, please get it in writing—commonly called a "letter of offer/intent." In addition to salary, each item negotiated should be spelled out clearly. It should also include a start date. A copy of the "letter of offer/intent" would need to be signed and returned by the due date. Then it becomes a legal document.

IN SUMMARY

For a quick review, here are the key concepts covered:

- Show respect and fairness—win/win

- Negotiating involves compromises and some risk taking

- Research and know your salary range

- Be willing to accept your minimum in your salary range

- Try to get them to give the salary or salary range first

- Use vagueness to your advantage

- Have several alternate plans if negotiations become tough

- Get it in writing

- Sign and return a copy

- Expect a successful negotiation

So there you have it! Now you can get the job that you have been wanting and get paid what you are worth!

11

HOW FRIENDS CAN HELP

UNDERSTANDING UNEMPLOYMENT

Many people lose their finances, their identity and their social life when they lose their job. It is traumatic and even well-educated and responsible people can be left bruised and badly shaken. People really do not know what unemployment means is until they become unemployed themselves. It cuts across social, economic, racial, religious and educational lines.

Your time is your own . . . so is the park bench.

So what can a supportive friend do to help an unemployed buddy? Some may tell a friend that he is sorry that you lost your job, give a word of encouragement, maybe say a little prayer and then send you off to the unemployment office (much of the paperwork is now done by the Internet and by phone). The unemployment office is a logical place to start even though it can feel very humiliating. The unemployed person, however, needs much more help than what the unemployment office has to offer. Whatever the amount, it is not going to meet the financial needs of your friend. You will usually need more than financial assistance. You will need guidance to search for a job. You will likely need help to cope with your emotions, worries, spiritual and intellectual issues. Most of this guidance will not come from an unemployment office. A friend can and should be a resource for a variety of your needs.

There are many different phases and moods that people go through when they lose their jobs. People can be elated, cocky or terrified, while some respond with little apparent emotional change. Even though there are a wide variety of responses, there are three initial dominant ones. They are isolation, depression and self-blame. The average time is 2-6 months to find new employment. For each person who finds employment in one month there is another person who takes nine to ten months. Even a year to a year and a half is not uncommon. The unemployed tend to isolate themselves, seek solitude and unless someone in their social circle helps out, often stay invisible.

Depression plays a large part. It becomes difficult for the unemployed to be enthusiastic and upbeat at a job interview—especially, after 10 or 15 interviews and no offer has been made. It becomes a vicious cycle. They need love, guidance and acceptance to overcome the feeling of depression.

Self-blame may not be only a psychological issue but can also be spiritual. "I must have done something wrong" shapes a large portion of this kind of thinking. The idea that we are punished for our sins is deeply ingrained in many people.

A supportive friend can play a pivotal role as facilitator, counselor, guide, support and a valuable resource. There is an abundance of resources, if only the unemployed knew how to locate them. A friend can help point the way. There is free legal and even sometimes financial help. There are temporary ways to reduce mortgage payments. There are support groups, but where? This chapter is designed to assist friends to help guide their less fortunate pal to full employment. Most of these pointers are not expensive or time consuming but they can be very effective.

WHAT CAN A FRIEND DO?

Below is a list of opportunities that a friend can use to help. They are low cost but can be significant assets.

- Help provide resources where information can be obtained from a government agency, church or synagogue regarding spiritual, financial, emotional, physical and career counseling

- Research the possibilities where "reemployment workshops" or support groups are held on a regular basis

- Go over the five common misunderstandings (*See* Chapter 2—Coping)

- Borrow or buy books about coping and reemployment (*See* Additional Resources)

- Be a facilitator—bring together a number of friends to form a support group

- Refer your friend to qualified career and unemployment counselors

- Just be a true friend—you know what that means!

12

TEN WORK MYTHS

◆

(I was <u>Dumb</u> Enough to Believe!)

Which of these myths did you believe?

1. The more education, the higher the income

2. Doing an excellent job insures not being fired

3. Large corporations provide more job security

4. Success is climbing the corporate ladder

5. Bosses always know best

6. Creativity is rewarded

7. Working hard pays more dollars

8. Honesty is the best way to keep a job

9. Social Security will be enough for retirement

10. More overtime equals more job security

13

DRESS & IMAGE

First impressions count! Prospective employers associate our abilities and competence with our appearance—dress and image. Our dress and image can express confidence, competence, self-management, attention to detail and responsibility. Make it work for you!

Tips for Everyone

- Dress conservatively

- Dress to look and feel good

- Dress appropriately for the job

- Enlist clothiers—it's free and professional

- Use cologne/perfume sparingly

- Use breath fresheners

Especially for Women

- Suit, blouse and accessories should match

- Bring purse or attaché—*not* both

- Use jewelry and makeup sparingly

- Have hair professionally styled to enhance your professional image

- Nails—avoid designs and dark colors, use clear or tinted polish

Especially for Men

- Shirt, suit and tie should match and compliment

- Belted pants or suspenders

- Use jewelry sparingly and hide tattoos

- Avoid long hair

- Nails clean and trimmed

14

KEEPING TRACK

It is always important to keep track of your contacts and activities. Below are a variety of forms to assist you along the way. Don't feel obligated to use all the forms but I strongly suggest that you use some of them. After many contacts, names and places begin to blur. They are designed to be photocopied as needed.

MY NEXT JOB

CHECK LIST   Name _____

Assessment
- ☐ Completed all the testing/measuring instruments necessary
- ☐ Decided to look in a specific direction or category of jobs

Resume
- ☐ Completed the traditional resume(s)
- ☐ Completed a scannable resume in text or ASCII format
- ☐ Posted my resume on the Internet
- ☐ Emailed resume to people who requested it and to friends, etc.
- ☐ Completed my references sheet (including permission)
- ☐ Composed a rough draft outline for a cover letter

Networking
- ☐ Wrote out "Introduction" statement
- ☐ Wrote out "Tell Me More" statement
- ☐ Filled out "My Networking" list
- ☐ Began in earnest to work through "My Networking" list
- ☐ Filled out "My Company Contact" list
- ☐ Began to use "My Company Contact" list
- ☐ Formed a small group to meet each week for support and ideas
- ☐ Ordered business cards

Internet
- ☐ Began in earnest to apply for jobs on the Internet

Agencies
- ☐ Contacted recruiters
- ☐ Contacted employment agencies

Job Fairs
- ☐ Researched and scheduled for at least three job fairs

Interviewing
- ☐ Know my worth and salary range through research on the Internet
- ☐ Have a clear bottom line or minimum in salary and benefits
- ☐ Wrote out answers to all my interview questions
- ☐ Wrote out two examples for each behavioral interview question
- ☐ Practiced interview questions with someone I trust and who can mentor me
- ☐ Developed a list of options/alternatives to negotiate salary, etc.
- ☐ Developed a list of questions that focus on my values/concerns

ACTIVITY LOG

DATE	NAME	ACTIVITY

TELEPHONE LOG

Date/Time	NAME	TEL. #	NOTES

POCKET
INTERVIEW CHECKLIST

PREPARATION
  • Ask for a job description (if possible)
  • Write out and practice interview questions
  • Research company
  • Visit site in advance (if possible)
  • Dress/Grooming (clean body, clothes,
        breath, car, etc.)

WHAT TO BRING
  • Copies of your resume and reference sheet
  • Information sheet/other job application
        (filled out)
  • Pen and a spare (blue/black ink only)
  • Notepad
  • Mints/breath freshener
  • Dress (equal or one step up)
  • Light reading (magazine, etc.)

ARRIVAL
  • Arrive early (½ hour grace time)
  • Check grooming/hair in restroom
  • Calming exercises (as needed)
  • Pop a breath freshener

(over)

FRONT

Photocopy, cut and glue/tape to copy on next page:

(Continued)
INTERVIEW CHECKLIST

OUTER OFFICE
- Establish rapport
- First impressions most important
    (including the receptionist)
- Fill out forms completely, N/A, etc.
- Look at a magazine/light reading
    (no newspapers)

ACTUAL INTERVIEW
- Be genuine (not a performance)
- 30-45 seconds (average length of answer)
- Lead conversation toward challenges/
    solutions by asking questions
- Find out employers expectations early
    (just ask)
- Ask questions but not too many
    (use cheat sheet)

FOLLOW-UP
- Thank secretary/receptionist for their help.
- Send a thank you note immediately
- Emphasize one key item (if at all)
- Tone and enthusiasm are crucial

BACK

Photocopy, cut and glue/tape to copy of previous page:

INTERVIEW SELF-EVALUATION

Fill out after each inverview to improve your interviewing skills.

Place _____ Date _____

How well did I do on this interview?

Circle one for each	Excellent		Average		Needs Improvement
Researching the company	5	4	3	2	1
Dress and image	5	4	3	2	1
Poise and confidence	5	4	3	2	1
Answering questions	5	4	3	2	1
Asking questions	5	4	3	2	1
Pursuing their needs	5	4	3	2	1

TOTAL SCORE _____ $\div$ 6 = _____ Average score

Suggested improvements: _____

_____

_____

_____

_____

Make photocopies

ADDITIONAL RESOURCES

Below are a few books that you might find helpful. They are popular books that can usually be purchased at a national bookstore or on the Internet at www.amazon.com.

ASSESSMENT & CAREER DECISION MAKING

Finding Your Own North Star *(Claiming the Life You Were Meant To Live)*, Martha Beck, Three Rivers Press.

Life Launch *(A Passionate Guide to the Rest of Your Life)*, Frederic Hudson and Pamela McLean, The Hudson Institute Press.

Soul Work (Finding the Work You Love, Loving the Work You Have), Deborah Block and Lee Richmond, Davies-Black Publishing.

Switching Careers *(Career Changes Tell How—and Why—They Did It, Learn How You Can too)*, Robert K. Otterbourg, Kiplinger Books.

The Pathfinder *(How to Choose or Change Your Career for a Lifetime of Satisfaction and Success)*, Nicholas Lore, Simon & Schuster.

The Power of Purpose *(Creating Meaning in Your Life and Work)*, Richard Leider, Berrett-Koehler Publishers, Inc.

What Brings You to Life? *(Awakening Woman's Spiritual Essence)*, Beverly Eanes, Lee Richmond and Jean Link, Paulist Press.

What Should I Do With My Life? Po Bronson, Random House.

Whistle While You Work *(Heeding Your Life's Calling)*, Richard Leider and David Shapiro, Berrett-Koehler Publishers.

Wishcraft *(How to Get What You Really Want)*, Barbara Sher, Ballantine Books.

RESUME

Resume Winners From The Pros *(177 of the Best from the Professional Association of Resume Writers)*, Wendy S. Enelow, Impact Publications.

The Resume Catalog: 200 Damn Good Examples, Yana Parker, Ten Speed Press.

NETWORKING

52 Ways To Re-connect, Follow Up, & Stay in Touch…, Anne Baber and Lynne Waymon, Kendall/Hunt Publishing.

Smart Networking *(How to Turn Contacts into Cash, Clients and Career Success)*, Anne Baber and Lynne Waymon, Kendall/Hunt Publishing.

Power Networking (59 Secrets for Personal & Professional Success), Donna Fisher and Sandy Vilas, Bard Press.

INTERVIEWING

Get Hired, Paul C. Green, Bard Press.

The Interview Rehearsal Book *(7 Steps to Job-Winning Interviews Using Acting Skills You Never Knew You Had)*, Deb Gottesman and Buzz Mauro, Berkley Books.

NEGOTIATING

101 Salary Secrets: How to Negotiate Like a Pro, Daniel Porot, Ten Speed Press.

Dynamite Salary Negotiations, Ronald L. Krannich, Impact Publications.

Get More Money on Your Next Job *(25 Proven Strategies for Getting More Money, Better Benefits and Greater Job Security)*, Lee Miller, McGraw-Hill Trade.

Get Paid What Your *Worth* *(The Expert Negotiators' Guide to Salary and Compensation)*, Robin Pinkley and Gregory Northcraft, Griffin Trade Paperback.

GENERAL STRATEGY

Coach Yourself to Success *(101 Tips from a Personal Coach for Reaching Your Goals)*, Talane Miedanes, Contemporary Books.

Dancing Naked *(Breaking Through the Emotional Limits that Keep You from the Job You Want)*, Robert Chope, New Harbinger Publications.

Don't Send A Resume *(And Other Contrarian Rules to Help Land a Great Job)*, Jeffrey J. Fox, Hyperion.

How To Fire Proof Your Career *(Survival Strategies for Volatile Time)*, Anne Baber and Lynn Waymon, Berkley Books.

lifeworktransitions.com *(Putting Your Spirit Online)*, Deborah Knox and Sandra Butzel, Butterworth Heinemann.

Repacking Your Bags *(Lighten Your Load for the Rest of Your Life)*, Richard Leider and David Shapiro, Berrett-Koehler Publishers.

The Career Coach *(Winning Strategies for Getting Ahead in Today's Job Market)*, Gordon Miller, Currency-Doubleday.

Turbulent Change *(Every Working Person's Survival Guide)*, Peter Garber, Davies-Black Publishing.

About the Author

Marvin Adams' involvement in training and development spans more than two decades. His consulting practice pivots around professional assistance to corporations, governmental agencies and individuals. Specializing in career development and coaching, his innovative and creative ways of problem solving are much in demand. Marvin works with groups or individuals with the same ease. His career also bridges both the corporate and academic worlds. He serves as an adjunct faculty member on two colleges campuses. The courses he teaches include: Career Decision Making and Business Ethics.

Marvin graduated from Bowie State University, summa cum laude, with a masters degree in counseling psychology. He also holds a theology degree from Columbia Union College. He currently holds certifications in the following:

> CCM—Credentialed Career Master
> JCDC—Job and Career Development Coach
> GCDF—Global Career Development Facilitator (and Instructor)
> SSI—Strong Interest Inventory®
> MBTI—Myers-Briggs Type Indicator Step II®

He also holds membership in:

> ACA—American Counseling Association
> MCDA—Maryland Career Development Association
> CMI—Career Masters Institute
> ASTD—American Society for Training and Development

He lives in suburban Maryland with his wife and cat.

0-595-31885-1